21 LEADERSHIP
ISSUES
IN THE
BIBLE

LIFE-CHANGING LESSONS
from LEADERS *in* SCRIPTURE

JOHN C.
MAXWELL

THOMAS NELSON
Since 1798

CONTENTS

ACKNOWLEDGMENTS

I want to say thank you to Charlie Wetzel and the rest of the team who assisted me with the formation and publication of this book. And to the people in my organizations who support it. You all add incredible value to me, which allows me to add value to others. Together, we're making a difference!

INTRODUCTION

Early in my career when I first began teaching people in church about leadership, they were often surprised. I was young and inexperienced, and the ideas I was able to convey seemed to be beyond what I should know. Later when I started writing about leadership, people gravitated to the message. And when I started writing and speaking to a more general audience, people used to ask, "Where in the world did you learn all this?"

I was happy to let them in on a secret: everything I know about leadership I learned from the Bible.

Not only is the Bible the greatest book ever written, it is the greatest *leadership* book ever written. Everything you could ever want to learn about leadership—vision, purpose, thinking strategy, communication, attitude, encouragement, mentoring, follow-through—is all there. You just need to be open to what God wants to teach you. As it says in Isaiah 55:11,

> *My word that goes out from my mouth:*
> *It will not return to me empty,*
> *but will accomplish what I desire*
> *and achieve the purpose for which I sent it.*

God's word always fulfills his purpose. If you have felt a stirring to become a better leader or if someone has tapped your shoulder and asked you to lead, God will help you.

I am excited for you as you begin this journey of leadership development through the Word of God. I've chosen 21 leadership issues that I believe every leader faces. I have included a brief excerpt from one of my books explaining the issue, and followed it with three carefully selected biblical case studies—some positive, some negative—that offer insight into the issue. After you read each of these passages from the Bible, you will answer study questions prompting you to really dig into the Scripture and learn about leadership from it.

This study guide is designed to be more than just a theoretical exercise. It's meant to help you *become* a better leader able to practice better leadership with others. To help facilitate that, you will be directed to reflect on how you can apply the leadership lessons to your own life. You will also develop a specific action item to help you follow through and improve your leadership.

You can easily go through this study guide on your own and improve your leadership ability. But I encourage you to do this with a group. There's nothing like learning with other like-minded people who desire to grow and develop their leadership skills. To help you with this process, I've included group discussion questions at the end of each lesson.

My recommendation is that you gather a group of people to engage in the process together. Before every meeting, each of you should complete the study questions, reflection, and action item on your own for that lesson. Then gather together as a group and answer the discussion questions and share what you've learned. I believe you'll find that you learn better and enjoy this process more in a group.

May God bless you as enjoy this journey.

IDENTITY

You Have Great Value Because God Values You

THE ISSUE DEFINED

You've probably heard people say, "You had to see it to believe it!" That's true in many situations. But when it comes to a person's potential, the opposite is actually true: they have to believe it in order to see it. Unfortunately, many of us don't see or cultivate the possibilities God put in us. Our low opinion of ourselves keeps us from believing we could ever blossom into something wonderful. That's unfortunate, because low self-esteem puts a ceiling on potential. If you want to achieve your leadership potential, you must value yourself as God values you.

You are valuable to God because of *who you are:* you were made in God's image, according to his likeness. You are valuable to him because of *what you cost:* even before you were born, Jesus gave everything to redeem you. You are valuable because of *what you can become:* before you took your first breath, God had a plan for you.

Accepting just how much God values us begins when we understand just how well he knows us. He knows everything about us, from before we were born until now. He sees all of our weaknesses, mistakes, and wrong motives. And he places the highest value on us anyway. In fact, he chooses to use us not in spite of our weaknesses, but because of them. As Paul says in 2 Corinthians 12:9, his "power is made perfect in weakness." God is glorified when we allow him to work through us.

Nothing can make someone more unlikely—even unwilling—to lead than feelings of inadequacy. But God doesn't choose leaders based only on their natural talent or ability. Neither does he choose them based on their age or experience. God chooses leaders based on their availability, not their ability; on their willingness to walk in obedience to him, not their own strength.

Leaders who see themselves through God's eyes are able to find their identity in him. This gives them confidence and courage. They become intentional about living a life that matches who they are by virtue of their relationship with Christ. As they discover and embrace their unique gifts, they are able to use those gifts to influence others and add value to their lives. Finally, as they accept and surrender their shortcomings, they begin a never-ending growth journey. They keep growing, keep making a difference in this world, and keep adding value to others' lives. You matter. You have value. Start living like it today and never stop.

CASE STUDIES

Read these case studies from the Bible and answer the study questions that follow.

❶ Gideon Is a Mighty Warrior—Because God Says So

Judges 6:11–40

¹¹ The angel of the Lᴏʀᴅ came and sat down under the oak in Ophrah that belonged to Joash the Abiezrite, where his son Gideon was threshing wheat in a winepress to keep it from the Midianites. ¹² When the angel of the Lᴏʀᴅ appeared to Gideon, he said, "The Lᴏʀᴅ is with you, mighty warrior."

¹³ "Pardon me, my lord," Gideon replied, "but if the Lᴏʀᴅ is with us, why has all this happened to us? Where are all his wonders that our ancestors told us about when they said, 'Did not the Lᴏʀᴅ bring us up out of Egypt?' But now the Lᴏʀᴅ has abandoned us and given us into the hand of Midian."

¹⁴ The Lᴏʀᴅ turned to him and said, "Go in the strength you have and save Israel out of Midian's hand. Am I not sending you?"

¹⁵ "Pardon me, my lord," Gideon replied, "but how can I save Israel? My clan is the weakest in Manasseh, and I am the least in my family."

¹⁶ The LORD answered, "I will be with you, and you will strike down all the Midianites, leaving none alive."

¹⁷ Gideon replied, "If now I have found favor in your eyes, give me a sign that it is really you talking to me. ¹⁸ Please do not go away until I come back and bring my offering and set it before you."

And the LORD said, "I will wait until you return."

¹⁹ Gideon went inside, prepared a young goat, and from an ephah of flour he made bread without yeast. Putting the meat in a basket and its broth in a pot, he brought them out and offered them to him under the oak.

²⁰ The angel of God said to him, "Take the meat and the unleavened bread, place them on this rock, and pour out the broth." And Gideon did so. ²¹ Then the angel of the LORD touched the meat and the unleavened bread with the tip of the staff that was in his hand. Fire flared from the rock, consuming the meat and the bread. And the angel of the LORD disappeared. ²² When Gideon realized that it was the angel of the LORD, he exclaimed, "Alas, Sovereign LORD! I have seen the angel of the LORD face to face!"

²³ But the LORD said to him, "Peace! Do not be afraid. You are not going to die."

²⁴ So Gideon built an altar to the LORD there and called it The LORD Is Peace. To this day it stands in Ophrah of the Abiezrites.

²⁵ That same night the LORD said to him, "Take the second bull from your father's herd, the one seven years old. Tear down your father's altar to Baal and cut down the Asherah pole beside it. ²⁶ Then build a proper kind of altar to the LORD your God on the top of this height. Using the wood of the Asherah pole that you cut down, offer the second bull as a burnt offering."

²⁷ So Gideon took ten of his servants and did as the LORD told him. But because he was afraid of his family and the townspeople, he did it at night rather than in the daytime.

²⁸ In the morning when the people of the town got up, there was Baal's altar, demolished, with the Asherah pole beside it cut down and the second bull sacrificed on the newly built altar!

²⁹ They asked each other, "Who did this?"

When they carefully investigated, they were told, "Gideon son of Joash did it."

³⁰ The people of the town demanded of Joash, "Bring out your son. He must die, because he has broken down Baal's altar and cut down the Asherah pole beside it."

³¹ But Joash replied to the hostile crowd around him, "Are you going to plead Baal's cause? Are you trying to save him? Whoever fights for him shall be put to death by morning! If Baal really is a god, he can defend himself when someone breaks down his altar." ³² So because Gideon broke down Baal's altar, they gave him the name Jerub-Baal that day, saying, "Let Baal contend with him."

³³ Now all the Midianites, Amalekites and other eastern peoples joined forces and crossed over the Jordan and camped in the Valley of Jezreel. ³⁴ Then the Spirit of the Lord came on Gideon, and he blew a trumpet, summoning the Abiezrites to follow him. ³⁵ He sent messengers throughout Manasseh, calling them to arms, and also into Asher, Zebulun and Naphtali, so that they too went up to meet them.

³⁶ Gideon said to God, "If you will save Israel by my hand as you have promised—³⁷ look, I will place a wool fleece on the threshing floor. If there is dew only on the fleece and all the ground is dry, then I will know that you will save Israel by my hand, as you said." ³⁸ And that is what happened. Gideon rose early the next day; he squeezed the fleece and wrung out the dew— a bowlful of water.

³⁹ Then Gideon said to God, "Do not be angry with me. Let me make just one more request. Allow me one more test with the fleece, but this time make the fleece dry and let the ground be covered with dew." ⁴⁰ That night God did so. Only the fleece was dry; all the ground was covered with dew.

Study Questions

1. Gideon's account opens with him threshing wheat in a winepress to keep it from the Midianites. What does that say about his leadership at that time?

   _____

   _____

   _____

   _____

   _____

2. The angel of the Lord addresses Gideon as "mighty warrior." What does his response to the angel say about Gideon's view of himself? How does he describe himself?

_____

_____

_____

_____

3. When Gideon saw the angel cause the meat and bread to be consumed by fire, he came to the realization that he had seen the angel of the Lord face to face. Why, then, did he ask God to verify his calling twice with the fleece?

_____

_____

_____

_____

4. Why do you think Gideon's doubt was so strong?

_____

_____

_____

_____

② God Knows Us Completely

Psalm 139:1–24

¹ *You have searched me, LORD,*
    and you know me.
² *You know when I sit and when I rise;*
    you perceive my thoughts from afar.
³ *You discern my going out and my lying down;*
    you are familiar with all my ways.
⁴ *Before a word is on my tongue*
    you, LORD, know it completely.

⁵ You hem me in behind and before,
and you lay your hand upon me.
⁶ Such knowledge is too wonderful for me,
too lofty for me to attain.

⁷ Where can I go from your Spirit?
Where can I flee from your presence?
⁸ If I go up to the heavens, you are there;
if I make my bed in the depths, you are there.
⁹ If I rise on the wings of the dawn,
if I settle on the far side of the sea,
¹⁰ even there your hand will guide me,
your right hand will hold me fast.
¹¹ If I say, "Surely the darkness will hide me
and the light become night around me,"
¹² even the darkness will not be dark to you;
the night will shine like the day,
for darkness is as light to you.

¹³ For you created my inmost being;
you knit me together in my mother's womb.
¹⁴ I praise you because I am fearfully and wonderfully made;
your works are wonderful,
I know that full well.
¹⁵ My frame was not hidden from you
when I was made in the secret place,
when I was woven together in the depths of the earth.
¹⁶ Your eyes saw my unformed body;
all the days ordained for me were written in your book
before one of them came to be.
¹⁷ How precious to me are your thoughts, God!
How vast is the sum of them!
¹⁸ Were I to count them,
they would outnumber the grains of sand—
when I awake, I am still with you.

¹⁹ If only you, God, would slay the wicked!
*   Away from me, you who are bloodthirsty!*
²⁰ They speak of you with evil intent;
*   your adversaries misuse your name.*
²¹ Do I not hate those who hate you, LORD,
*   and abhor those who are in rebellion against you?*
²² I have nothing but hatred for them;
*   I count them my enemies.*
²³ Search me, God, and know my heart;
*   test me and know my anxious thoughts.*
²⁴ See if there is any offensive way in me,
*   and lead me in the way everlasting.*

Study Questions

1. How many different ways in this Psalm does David express the idea that God knows him? List them.

_____

_____

_____

_____

_____

_____

_____

_____

_____

_____

2. How would you describe David's response to this knowledge? How does it impact him?

_____

_____

_____

_____

_____

3. How does David's view differ from the way most people see God?

_____

_____

_____

_____

_____

_____

❸ Peter's Sense of Identity Gives Him Confidence

Acts 4:1–20

¹ *The priests and the captain of the temple guard and the Sadducees came up to Peter and John while they were speaking to the people.* ² *They were greatly disturbed because the apostles were teaching the people, proclaiming in Jesus the resurrection of the dead.* ³ *They seized Peter and John and, because it was evening, they put them in jail until the next day.* ⁴ *But many who heard the message believed; so the number of men who believed grew to about five thousand.*

⁵ *The next day the rulers, the elders and the teachers of the law met in Jerusalem.* ⁶ *Annas the high priest was there, and so were Caiaphas, John, Alexander and others of the high priest's family.* ⁷ *They had Peter and John brought before them and began to question them: "By what power or what name did you do this?"*

⁸ *Then Peter, filled with the Holy Spirit, said to them: "Rulers and elders of the people!* ⁹ *If we are being called to account today for an act of kindness shown to a man who was lame and are being asked how he was healed,* ¹⁰ *then know this, you and all the people of Israel: It is by the name of Jesus Christ of Nazareth, whom you crucified but whom God raised from the dead, that this man stands before you healed.* ¹¹ *Jesus is*

> *'the stone you builders rejected,*
> *which has become the cornerstone.'*

¹² *Salvation is found in no one else, for there is no other name under heaven given to mankind by which we must be saved."*

13 When they saw the courage of Peter and John and realized that they were unschooled, ordinary men, they were astonished and they took note that these men had been with Jesus. 14 But since they could see the man who had been healed standing there with them, there was nothing they could say. 15 So they ordered them to withdraw from the Sanhedrin and then conferred together. 16 "What are we going to do with these men?" they asked. "Everyone living in Jerusalem knows they have performed a notable sign, and we cannot deny it. 17 But to stop this thing from spreading any further among the people, we must warn them to speak no longer to anyone in this name."

18 Then they called them in again and commanded them not to speak or teach at all in the name of Jesus. 19 But Peter and John replied, "Which is right in God's eyes: to listen to you, or to him? You be the judges! 20 As for us, we cannot help speaking about what we have seen and heard."

Study Questions

1. What is the significance of the description of Peter and John as being "unschooled, ordinary men"?

_____

_____

_____

_____

2. What role do you think identity played in Peter and John's boldness in speaking, healing people, and standing up to the high priest and other officials?

_____

_____

_____

_____

3. What role did evidence and results play in this interaction?

_____

_____

_____

_____

4. How difficult do you think it was for Peter and John to defy the Sanhedrin and say that they would listen to God, not them? What gave them the confidence to do this? Why didn't the officials do more to stop them?

_____

_____

_____

_____

Leadership Insight and Reflection

In what ways were the identities of Gideon, David, and Peter established by God? How did they differ? What did they have in common?

_____

_____

_____

_____

_____

Where did each leader's identity come from?

_____

_____

_____

_____

_____

Taking Action

Think about your sense of identity. Where does it come from? Describe yourself by writing a list of personally descriptive statements. In parentheses next to each statement, write a word indicating the source or origin of that idea about yourself.

_____

_____

_____

_____

_____

_____

_____

Now write a paragraph about yourself attempting to see yourself from God's point of view. How do you think *he* would describe you?

_____

_____

_____

_____

_____

_____

_____

What differences do you see in the two descriptions? What strengths, gifts, or talents do you possess that could help you be a better leader?

_____

_____

_____

_____

_____

_____

_____

What do you believe God would like you to do to reinforce your identity based on how God created you and how he sees you?

_____

_____

_____

_____

_____

_____

_____

Group Discussion Questions

1. How might Gideon's life have played out differently if the angel hadn't told him he was a mighty warrior?

2. Gideon obeyed the angel, but he did so at night. How do you interpret this action? Was it cowardice? Was it full obedience? Was it a good intermediate step? Or would you describe it another way?

3. What strikes you most about what David wrote in Psalm 139?

4. Do you identify with the way David thought about God, or is your thinking different from his? Explain.

5. What actions taken by Peter and John in the Acts passage indicate a strong sense of identity? How did their strong sense of identity positively impact their leadership?

6. Based on what you read in the three passages, in what ways could your sense of identity stand to improve? Explain.

7. What can you do to better connect with God and strengthen your sense of identity? When and how will you follow through with this?

SURRENDER

Submit to God's Authority
Before Trying to Develop Yours

THE ISSUE DEFINED

You may be wondering how *surrender* could be a leadership issue. Doesn't leadership require strength while surrender shows weakness? Not necessarily. Surrender actually shows cooperation, especially when you're discussing submission to authority. That's often referred to as followership, and it is something *all* leaders need to know how to do, especially leaders of faith.

As a Christian leader, you are asked to make the choice to surrender to the highest authority, i.e. God. Why is this important? First, God makes it clear throughout the Bible that he expects and requires it of us. Accepting Christ is a surrender of self. Second, God has clearly promised to bless our actions and decisions when they are fully surrendered to his will. When we submit to him, it allows him to work through us to achieve his purposes.

Humility is necessary for surrender to God. It means acknowledging that he is, was, and always will be our leader. As the most powerful entity ever, he created everyone and everything. He exists outside of time. And he's the source of every believer's power and success. When God's leaders choose to acknowledge God's sovereignty and submit 100 percent, God fills their leadership with his power and authority. And his leaders are able to achieve much more than they ever could on their own.

Surrender to God also requires trust in his goodness. Besides believing that he is always able to do great things in and through us, we must believe that he always desires to do what's best for us. Lack of trust in God is often at the root of a lack of submission. After all, why would anyone willingly give their allegiance to someone they can't trust? Christian leaders who choose to trust God's love and motives are able to give him their total allegiance. And he empowers them to lead out of a desire to benefit their people.

The bottom line is there's no such thing as partially surrendering or sharing credit with God. Wise leaders remember that God is the one who gives any power or success they might enjoy. And they recognize that when God asks us to do something, our response is yes. And from that place of submission to him, we learn to lead others.

CASE STUDIES

Read these case studies from the Bible and answer the study questions that follow.

① Surrender and Trust Go Hand in Hand

Proverbs 3:1–12

¹ My son, do not forget my teaching,
   but keep my commands in your heart,
      ² for they will prolong your life many years
      and bring you peace and prosperity.

³ Let love and faithfulness never leave you;
   bind them around your neck,
   write them on the tablet of your heart.
      ⁴ Then you will win favor and a good name
      in the sight of God and man.

5 *Trust in the LORD with all your heart*
    and lean not on your own understanding;
    6 *in all your ways submit to him,*
    and he will make your paths straight.

7 *Do not be wise in your own eyes;*
    fear the LORD and shun evil.
    8 *This will bring health to your body*
    and nourishment to your bones.

9 *Honor the LORD with your wealth,*
    with the firstfruits of all your crops;
    10 *then your barns will be filled to overflowing,*
    and your vats will brim over with new wine.

11 *My son, do not despise the LORD's discipline,*
    and do not resent his rebuke,
    12 *because the LORD disciplines those he loves,*
    as a father the son he delights in.

Study Questions

1. Describe the positive relationship with God that the Proverbs writer paints for his son. What are its characteristics? What is its value to the son?

_____

_____

_____

_____

_____

_____

_____

_____

_____

_____

_____

2. Why is trust so important to this relationship? What happens when it's absent?

_____

_____

_____

_____

_____

_____

_____

3. How is honoring the Lord with one's wealth a sign of surrender?

_____

_____

_____

_____

_____

4. Why does the Proverbs writer tell his son to accept the Lord's discipline? How is that related to surrender and trust?

_____

_____

_____

_____

_____

_____

_____

❷ God Requires and Blesses Humble Surrender

James 3:13–18

13 Who is wise and understanding among you? Let them show it by their good life, by deeds done in the humility that comes from wisdom. 14 But if you harbor bitter envy and selfish ambition in your hearts, do not boast about it or deny the truth. 15 Such "wisdom" does not come down from heaven but is earthly, unspiritual, demonic. ¹⁶ For where you have envy and selfish ambition, there you find disorder and every evil practice.

¹⁷ But the wisdom that comes from heaven is first of all pure; then peace-loving, considerate, submissive, full of mercy and good fruit, impartial and sincere.¹⁸ Peacemakers who sow in peace reap a harvest of righteousness.

James 4:1–7

¹ What causes fights and quarrels among you? Don't they come from your desires that battle within you? ² You desire but do not have, so you kill. You covet but you cannot get what you want, so you quarrel and fight. You do not have because you do not ask God. ³ When you ask, you do not receive, because you ask with wrong motives, that you may spend what you get on your pleasures.

⁴ You adulterous people, don't you know that friendship with the world means enmity against God? Therefore, anyone who chooses to be a friend of the world becomes an enemy of God. ⁵ Or do you think Scripture says without reason that he jealously longs for the spirit he has caused to dwell in us?⁶ But he gives us more grace. That is why Scripture says:

> *"God opposes the proud*
> *but shows favor to the humble."*

⁷ Submit yourselves, then, to God. Resist the devil, and he will flee from you.

Study Questions

1. Why does James say that wisdom and humility are linked? Describe how they are related to one another.

   _____

   _____

   _____

   _____

   _____

   _____

2. Envy and selfish ambition could be described as characteristics that drive those who are not surrendered to God. How does James describe the lives of such people? How does that differ from someone characterized by wisdom?

_____

_____

_____

_____

_____

_____

_____

3. What does James say are the sources of people's fights and quarrels? How do fights and quarrels impact relationships? How do they impact leadership?

_____

_____

_____

_____

_____

4. James says the solution to pride and selfish ambition is to submit to God and resist the devil. How would that look in your life?

_____

_____

_____

_____

_____

❸ A Life Characterized by Surrender to God

1 Peter 2:1–25

¹ Therefore, rid yourselves of all malice and all deceit, hypocrisy, envy, and slander of every kind. ² Like newborn babies, crave pure spiritual milk, so that *by it you may grow up in your salvation, ³ now that you have tasted that the Lord is good.*

⁴ As you come to him, the living Stone—rejected by humans but chosen by God and precious to him— ⁵ you also, like living stones, are being built into a spiritual house to be a holy priesthood, offering spiritual sacrifices acceptable to God through Jesus Christ. ⁶ For in Scripture it says:

> *"See, I lay a stone in Zion,*
> > *a chosen and precious cornerstone,*
> *and the one who trusts in him*
> > *will never be put to shame."*

⁷ Now to you who believe, this stone is precious. But to those who do not believe,

> *"The stone the builders rejected*
> > *has become the cornerstone,"*

⁸ and,

> *"A stone that causes people to stumble*
> > *and a rock that makes them fall."*

They stumble because they disobey the message—which is also what they were destined for.

⁹ But you are a chosen people, a royal priesthood, a holy nation, God's special possession, that you may declare the praises of him who called you out of darkness into his wonderful light. ¹⁰ Once you were not a people, but now you are the people of God; once you had not received mercy, but now you have received mercy.

¹¹ Dear friends, I urge you, as foreigners and exiles, to abstain from sinful desires, which wage war against your soul. ¹² Live such good lives among the pagans that, though they accuse you of doing wrong, they may see your good deeds and glorify God on the day he visits us.

¹³ Submit yourselves for the Lord's sake to every human authority: whether to the emperor, as the supreme authority, ¹⁴ or to governors, who are sent by him to punish those who do wrong and to commend those who do right. *15 For it is God's will that by doing good you should silence the ignorant talk of foolish people.16 Live as free people, but do not use your freedom as a cover-up for evil; live as God's slaves. 17 Show proper respect to everyone, love the family of believers, fear God, honor the emperor.*

18 Slaves, in reverent fear of God submit yourselves to your masters, not only to those who are good and considerate, but also to those who are harsh. 19 For it is commendable if someone bears up under the pain of unjust suffering because they are conscious of God. 20 But how is it to your credit if you receive a beating for doing wrong and endure it? But if you suffer for doing good and you endure it, this is commendable before God. 21 To this you were called, because Christ suffered for you, leaving you an example, that you should follow in his steps.

> *22 "He committed no sin,*
> *and no deceit was found in his mouth."*

23 When they hurled their insults at him, he did not retaliate; when he suffered, he made no threats. Instead, he entrusted himself to him who judges justly. 24 "He himself bore our sins" in his body on the cross, so that we might die to sins and live for righteousness; "by his wounds you have been healed." 25 For "you were like sheep going astray," but now you have returned to the Shepherd and Overseer of your souls.

Study Questions

1. Peter uses the metaphor of a house being built to describe the spiritual growth process among believers. What kind of conduct paves the way for this kind of growth? What causes people to stumble in this process? What is the implication for leaders?

_____

_____

_____

_____

_____

_____

2. Peter spends quite a bit of time admonishing people to submit to human authorities. Why do you think he does this? Why is doing this important to us as followers of Christ and as leaders?

_____

_____

_____

_____

_____

_____

_____

_____

_____

_____

3. Why does Peter admonish believers to submit to unjust treatment?

_____

_____

_____

_____

_____

_____

_____

4. Peter says that Jesus "entrusted himself to him who judges justly" and advises us to do the same. What leadership lesson can you learn from this advice?

_____

_____

_____

_____

_____

_____

_____

_____

_____

_____

LEADERSHIP INSIGHT AND REFLECTION

Think about the importance of trust, humility, and wisdom in surrendering to God and authority. Describe the role that each plays in the process.

_____

_____

_____

_____

_____

_____

_____

_____

_____

_____

Which of those three qualities do you find most difficult to embody? Explain.

_____

_____

_____

_____

_____

_____

_____

_____

_____

What have you not surrendered to God that you believe he would like you to?

_____

_____

_____

_____

_____

_____

_____

_____

_____

How would surrender make you a better follower of Christ? How would it prepare you for leadership or make you a better leader?

_____

_____

_____

_____

_____

_____

TAKING ACTION

What must you do to surrender to God in this area?

_____

_____

_____

_____

_____

What is currently holding you back?

_____

_____

_____

_____

_____

What first step can you take immediately? If you need to ask for help from a trusted advisor or friend, do so. When will you take it?

_____

_____

_____

_____

_____

_____

GROUP DISCUSSION QUESTIONS

1. The Proverbs writer admonishes his son to trust God with all his heart and not rely on his own understanding. Why do people find that difficult to do? Where and why do you find it difficult?

2. James writes about "bitter envy and selfish ambition." Can envy ever be a positive force? Can ambition? Explain.

3. James writes, "You do not have because you do not ask God. When you ask, you do not receive, because you ask with wrong motives" What should leaders ask God for, and what motives would be right?

4. Peter says, "Submit yourself for the Lord's sake to every human authority." How difficult do you find that to do? Explain.

5. Is the term *surrender* typically seen as a strength or a weakness in most contexts? Why are followers of Christ asked to practice it?

6. What is the role of surrender in followership? How does your willingness to surrender help you as a leader?

7. Where is God is asking you grow and learn when it comes to surrender? What are you prepared to do to learn the lesson? When and how will you do it?

LESSON 3

PURPOSE

You Were Created for a Reason

THE ISSUE DEFINED

Has your life ever felt like a treadmill? Or maybe a hamster wheel? Like you are running but not really getting anywhere? Does it make you want to quit because there doesn't seem to be a point to what you're doing? In today's hectic world, it's easy to get caught up in activity, but activity is not necessarily accomplishment. No one ever got anywhere on a treadmill. And after a while, all that movement begins to feel meaningless.

The good news is that we were all made for more. You were created for something. God designed you with a purpose. Ephesians 2:10 says, "For we are God's handiwork, created in Christ Jesus to do good works, which God prepared in advance for us to do."

When people find and follow their purpose, they *know* their life has a point. A purpose points the way, clarifies priorities, and measures progress. By seeking and then acting on purpose, we find meaning and fulfillment. And God's will is achieved on earth.

So how do you find your unique purpose? First, look to God's word. His unique purpose for someone will always align with his big-picture purpose for all believers. Anything not aligned with God's principles is not from God.

Next, consider your current opportunities, abilities, and passions. God often uses these things, along with his supernatural guidance, to help us discover direction. In fact, one often leads to another: You may notice a need, then recognize you have a skill or gift that could be used to meet that need. You feel a desire to participate in the solution. And God stirs your heart with a call to take action. This *could* mean doing all the work to solve the problem alone, but it most frequently includes sharing the vision with others and leading people to solve it together.

Another sign that purpose comes from God is that it feels bigger than we are capable of doing. That's because a God-sized vision requires God's power. It's something we cannot and should not try to do on our own. But God always provides the supernatural power, wisdom, and resources necessary to achieve the goal when it's his. After we start following God's directions, he reveals more and more of the path ahead. And only then does he pour out the empowerment and resources that we need to do his will. And when we're done, God deserves all the glory.

People's passions and God's power combine to achieve God's purposes. Discovering God's calling and then pursuing it is like walking on a road, instead of a pointless treadmill. As we continue forward with God, he clears the way and sustains us on the journey. And we find true meaning and fulfillment in traveling with him.

CASE STUDIES

Read these case studies from the Bible and answer the study questions that follow.

❶ God's Purpose Is Fulfilled Through His Power

Psalm 33:1–22

> ¹ Sing joyfully to the LORD, you righteous;
> it is fitting for the upright to praise him.
> ² Praise the LORD with the harp;
> make music to him on the ten-stringed lyre.
> ³ Sing to him a new song;
> play skillfully, and shout for joy.

4 For the word of the Lord is right and true;
    he is faithful in all he does.
5 The Lord loves righteousness and justice;
    the earth is full of his unfailing love.

6 By the word of the Lord the heavens were made,
    their starry host by the breath of his mouth.
7 He gathers the waters of the sea into jars;
    he puts the deep into storehouses.
8 Let all the earth fear the Lord;
    let all the people of the world revere him.
9 For he spoke, and it came to be;
    he commanded, and it stood firm.

10 The Lord foils the plans of the nations;
    he thwarts the purposes of the peoples.
11 But the plans of the Lord stand firm forever,
    the purposes of his heart through all generations.

12 Blessed is the nation whose God is the Lord,
    the people he chose for his inheritance.
13 From heaven the Lord looks down
    and sees all mankind;
14 from his dwelling place he watches
    all who live on earth—
15 he who forms the hearts of all,
    who considers everything they do.

16 No king is saved by the size of his army;
    no warrior escapes by his great strength.
17 A horse is a vain hope for deliverance;
    despite all its great strength it cannot save.
18 But the eyes of the Lord are on those who fear him,
    on those whose hope is in his unfailing love,
19 to deliver them from death
    and keep them alive in famine.

²⁰ We wait in hope for the LORD;
  he is our help and our shield.
²¹ In him our hearts rejoice,
  for we trust in his holy name.
²² May your unfailing love be with us, LORD,
  even as we put our hope in you.

Study Questions

1. This Psalm speaks of God's faithfulness, righteousness, and power. How might those characteristics relate to his purpose for individual human beings? Can you connect them? Explain.

_____

_____

_____

_____

_____

_____

_____

_____

_____

2. The passage refers to the "plans of the Lord" and "the purposes of his heart through all generations." And it says that God "watches all who live on earth." Have you ever considered that these plans and purposes apply to you? What is your response to that?

_____

_____

_____

_____

_____

_____

_____

_____

3. Since God is described as having "unfailing love," what does that imply about his desires for you?

_____

_____

_____

_____

_____

_____

_____

_____

_____

_____

_____

_____

❷ God's Call Is Bigger Than Jeremiah Can Imagine

Jeremiah 1:1–19

1 The words of Jeremiah son of Hilkiah, one of the priests at Anathoth in the territory of Benjamin. 2 The word of the Lord came to him in the thirteenth year of the reign of Josiah son of Amon king of Judah, 3 and through the reign of Jehoiakim son of Josiah king of Judah, down to the fifth month of the eleventh year of Zedekiah son of Josiah king of Judah, when the people of Jerusalem went into exile.

4 The word of the Lord came to me, saying,

> *5 "Before I formed you in the womb I knew you,*
> *before you were born I set you apart;*
> *I appointed you as a prophet to the nations."*

6 "Alas, Sovereign Lord," I said, "I do not know how to speak; I am too young."
7 But the Lord said to me, "Do not say, 'I am too young.' You must go to everyone I send you to and say whatever I command you. 8 Do not be afraid of them, for I am with you and will rescue you," declares the Lord.

⁹ Then the Lord reached out his hand and touched my mouth and said to me, "I have put my words in your mouth. ¹⁰ See, today I appoint you over nations and kingdoms to uproot and tear down, to destroy and overthrow, to build and to plant."

¹¹ The word of the Lord came to me: "What do you see, Jeremiah?"

"I see the branch of an almond tree," I replied.

¹² The Lord said to me, "You have seen correctly, for I am watching to see that my word is fulfilled."

¹³ The word of the Lord came to me again: "What do you see?"

"I see a pot that is boiling," I answered. "It is tilting toward us from the north."

¹⁴ The Lord said to me, "From the north disaster will be poured out on all who live in the land. ¹⁵ I am about to summon all the peoples of the northern kingdoms," declares the Lord.

"Their kings will come and set up their thrones
in the entrance of the gates of Jerusalem;
they will come against all her surrounding walls
and against all the towns of Judah.
¹⁶ I will pronounce my judgments on my people
because of their wickedness in forsaking me,
in burning incense to other gods
and in worshiping what their hands have made.

¹⁷ "Get yourself ready! Stand up and say to them whatever I command you. Do not be terrified by them, or I will terrify you before them. ¹⁸ Today I have made you a fortified city, an iron pillar and a bronze wall to stand against the whole land—against the kings of Judah, its officials, its priests and the people of the land. ¹⁹ They will fight against you but will not overcome you, for I am with you and will rescue you," declares the Lord.

Study Questions

1. The passage says that God knew Jeremiah even before he was formed in the womb and that he set Jeremiah apart and appointed him as a prophet

even before he was born. Based on that information, what can you infer about God's relationship with people and whether people's purpose is discovered or chosen by them?

_____

_____

_____

_____

_____

_____

_____

_____

2. How important was maturity, experience, and skill to Jeremiah's calling and purpose?

_____

_____

_____

_____

_____

3. Would you consider the purpose God identified for Jeremiah be positive or negative for him personally? Explain.

_____

_____

_____

_____

_____

4. Twice God told Jeremiah that he was with him and would rescue him. Why do you think he communicated this?

_____

_____

_____

_____

_____

3 Saul's Passion, Transformed by God's Power, Fulfills God's Purpose

Acts 9:1–22

1 Meanwhile, Saul was still breathing out murderous threats against the Lord's disciples. He went to the high priest 2 and asked him for letters to the synagogues in Damascus, so that if he found any there who belonged to the Way, whether men or women, he might take them as prisoners to Jerusalem. 3 As he neared Damascus on his journey, suddenly a light from heaven flashed around him. 4 He fell to the ground and heard a voice say to him, "Saul, Saul, why do you persecute me?"

5 "Who are you, Lord?" Saul asked.

"I am Jesus, whom you are persecuting," he replied. 6 "Now get up and go into the city, and you will be told what you must do."

7 The men traveling with Saul stood there speechless; they heard the sound but did not see anyone. 8 Saul got up from the ground, but when he opened his eyes he could see nothing. So they led him by the hand into Damascus. 9 For three days he was blind, and did not eat or drink anything.

10 In Damascus there was a disciple named Ananias. The Lord called to him in a vision, "Ananias!"

"Yes, Lord," he answered.

11 The Lord told him, "Go to the house of Judas on Straight Street and ask for a man from Tarsus named Saul, for he is praying. 12 In a vision he has seen a man named Ananias come and place his hands on him to restore his sight."

13 "Lord," Ananias answered, "I have heard many reports about this man and all the harm he has done to your holy people in Jerusalem. 14 And he has come here with authority from the chief priests to arrest all who call on your name."

15 But the Lord said to Ananias, "Go! This man is my chosen instrument to proclaim my name to the Gentiles and their kings and to the people of Israel. 16 I will show him how much he must suffer for my name."

17 Then Ananias went to the house and entered it. Placing his hands on Saul, he said, "Brother Saul, the Lord—Jesus, who appeared to you on the road as you were coming here—has sent me so that you may see again and be filled with the Holy Spirit." 18 Immediately, something like scales fell from

Saul's eyes, and he could see again. He got up and was baptized, ¹⁹ and after taking some food, he regained his strength.

Saul spent several days with the disciples in Damascus. ²⁰ At once he began to preach in the synagogues that Jesus is the Son of God. ²¹ All those who heard him were astonished and asked, "Isn't he the man who raised havoc in Jerusalem among those who call on this name? And hasn't he come here to take them as prisoners to the chief priests?" ²² Yet Saul grew more and more powerful and baffled the Jews living in Damascus by proving that Jesus is the Messiah.

Study Questions

1. Based on this passage, how would you describe Saul's purpose before his encounter with Jesus on the road to Damascus? How would you describe his purpose after that encounter?

_____

_____

_____

_____

_____

2. Why do you think God afflicted Saul with temporary blindness?

_____

_____

_____

_____

3. Ananias also had an encounter with the Lord, being directed to go to Saul, whom he feared. What do you think would have happened if Ananias had refused to go to Saul?

_____

_____

_____

_____

4. How was it possible for Saul to change direction so quickly and only a few days after his encounter be able to preach that Jesus was the Son of God and prove he was the Messiah?

_____

_____

_____

_____

LEADERSHIP INSIGHT AND REFLECTION

The psalm says that God "thwarts the purposes of the peoples. But the plans of the Lord stand firm forever" (33:10–11). How did that play out for Jeremiah and Saul?

_____

_____

_____

_____

_____

Based on what you read in these passages, how are identity and purpose are related?

_____

_____

_____

_____

How do followers of Christ recognize when a purpose they are pursuing is their own and when it is from God?

_____

_____

_____

_____

_____

Describe what you currently believe to be your God-given purpose.

_____
_____
_____
_____
_____
_____
_____
_____

TAKING ACTION

Think about what you believe to be your purpose, and consider the following:

Does it align with Scripture?	❑ Yes	❑ No
Is it consistent with your identity?	❑ Yes	❑ No
Does it serve God and advance his kingdom?	❑ Yes	❑ No
Does it help other people?	❑ Yes	❑ No
Does it or will it glorify God?	❑ Yes	❑ No

If your answer to any of these questions is a clear no, you may need to prayerfully seek God for further direction and clarification.

What immediate step can you take toward fulfilling that purpose?

_____
_____
_____
_____
_____
_____

When will you do it? _____
_____

GROUP DISCUSSION QUESTIONS

1. In the past, have you believed that God has a specific purpose for your life? What about now? Explain.

2. God spoke clearly to Jeremiah about his purpose, and he appeared in person to Saul to give him direction. How can believers today find their God-given purpose?

3. Have you ever pursued a path of purpose in your life up to now? If so, describe it. If not, why not?

4. How has your sense of purpose or lack of purpose affected you emotionally, intellectually, relationally, and professionally?

5. Psalm 37:4 says, "Take delight in the Lord, and he will give you the desires of your heart." Do you believe that God's purpose for you and the desires of your heart can align? Explain your answer.

6. If you could experience significant movement forward in finding or fulfilling your purpose, what would you want it to be? Have you asked God about it?

7. What action could you take immediately—by yourself or with others— toward fulfilling your purpose? Will you take it? When?

LESSON 4

INTEGRITY

Bigger on the Inside Leads to Better on the Outside

THE ISSUE DEFINED

Integrity is defined as "the quality or the state of being complete; unbroken condition; wholeness; entirety." It means more than following a moral code. Its Latin root is the same as the word *integer*, a whole number. Wholeness is the opposite of being divided. When people focus more on developing their integrity than their image, they create a life that is whole. As they consistently keep their promises and practice what they preach, they become "bigger on the inside." In leaders, this creates trust, protects talent, and fosters internal peace.

In contrast, a focus on image over integrity is an attempt to appear bigger on the outside, often at the expense of who we are on the inside. This creates a cognitive dissonance, an unhealthy hypocrisy. Image might say something like, "What I say and what I do are not the same and never will be. That's the way it is. Just keep up appearances." That kind of thinking is especially bad for leaders, because it demonstrates that they're inauthentic, rationalizing, and unteachable.

Wise leaders establish integrity guardrails for themselves to keep from going off course. On a highway, guardrails keep cars from going over a cliff. The best guardrails are the decisions you make *before* you face high-pressure situations. For example, it's impossible to maintain integrity when you don't know what you value or where to draw the line. Do you value doing the right thing? Then what is your guardrail? What *won't* you do? Decide that before you face temptation. Do you value relationships? If so, what is your guardrail? What *must* you do to maintain your relationships? Identify your values and decide what boundaries you won't cross long before temptation comes.

When leaders focus on becoming bigger on the inside, in addition to benefitting their followers, they are caring for their own souls. A healthy soul is whole. It's not fractured. It holds together internally. Leaders of integrity also have self-respect, which comes not from accomplishments or achievements, but from making the right choices. And wholeness on the inside creates a more powerful outside. Another way to say it is that when you focus on image at the expense of integrity, you eventually lose both. But when you focus on maintaining integrity, the image that is created is authentic and trustworthy. And leadership influence grows from the inside out.

CASE STUDIES

Read these case studies from the Bible and answer the study questions that follow.

❶ Judah's Promise to Israel

Genesis 43:1–5, 8–9

¹ Now the famine was still severe in the land. ² So when they had eaten all the grain they had brought from Egypt, their father said to them, "Go back and buy us a little more food."

³ But Judah said to him, "The man warned us solemnly, 'You will not see my face again unless your brother is with you.' ⁴ If you will send our brother along with us, we will go down and buy food for you. ⁵ But if you will not send him, we will not go down, because the man said to us, 'You will not see my face again unless your brother is with you. . . .'"

⁸ Then Judah said to Israel his father, "Send the boy [Benjamin] along with me and we will go at once, so that we and you and our children may live and not die. ⁹ I myself will guarantee his safety; you can hold me personally responsible for him. If I do not bring him back to you and set him here before you, I will bear the blame before you all my life.

Genesis 44:18–34

18 Then Judah went up to him [the man, whom he didn't know was his brother Joseph] and said: "Pardon your servant, my lord, let me speak a word to my lord. Do not be angry with your servant, though you are equal to Pharaoh himself. 19 My lord asked his servants, 'Do you have a father or a brother?' 20 And we answered, 'We have an aged father, and there is a young son born to him in his old age. His brother is dead, and he is the only one of his mother's sons left, and his father loves him.'

21 "Then you said to your servants, 'Bring him down to me so I can see him for myself.' 22 And we said to my lord, 'The boy cannot leave his father; if he leaves him, his father will die.' 23 But you told your servants, 'Unless your youngest brother comes down with you, you will not see my face again.' 24 When we went back to your servant my father, we told him what my lord had said.

25 "Then our father said, 'Go back and buy a little more food.' 26 But we said, 'We cannot go down. Only if our youngest brother is with us will we go. We cannot see the man's face unless our youngest brother is with us.'

27 "Your servant my father said to us, 'You know that my wife bore me two sons. 28 One of them went away from me, and I said, "He has surely been torn to pieces." And I have not seen him since. 29 If you take this one from me too and harm comes to him, you will bring my gray head down to the grave in misery.'

30 "So now, if the boy is not with us when I go back to your servant my father, and if my father, whose life is closely bound up with the boy's life, 31 sees that the boy isn't there, he will die. Your servants will bring the gray head of our father down to the grave in sorrow. 32 Your servant guaranteed the boy's safety to my father. I said, 'If I do not bring him back to you, I will bear the blame before you, my father, all my life!'

33 "Now then, please let your servant remain here as my lord's slave in place of the boy, and let the boy return with his brothers. 34 How can I go back to my father if the boy is not with me? No! Do not let me see the misery that would come on my father."

Genesis 45:1–5

¹ *Then Joseph could no longer control himself before all his attendants, and he cried out, "Have everyone leave my presence!" So there was no one with Joseph when he made himself known to his brothers.* ² *And he wept so loudly that the Egyptians heard him, and Pharaoh's household heard about it.*

³ *Joseph said to his brothers, "I am Joseph! Is my father still living?" But his brothers were not able to answer him, because they were terrified at his presence.*

⁴ *Then Joseph said to his brothers, "Come close to me." When they had done so, he said, "I am your brother Joseph, the one you sold into Egypt!* ⁵ *And now, do not be distressed and do not be angry with yourselves for selling me here, because it was to save lives that God sent me ahead of you.'*

Study Questions

1. When the sons of Israel went to Egypt the first time to buy food, they had no idea they were dealing with their brother Joseph, whom they had sold into slavery many years before at the suggestion of Judah. Why do you think Judah offered to take responsibility for Benjamin before going back to Egypt for the second time?

   _____

   _____

   _____

   _____

   _____

2. On their second trip to Egypt recounted in this passage, Joseph set a trap for the brothers, making it look as if Benjamin had stolen a silver cup. When Joseph declared that Benjamin would become his slave, why do you think Judah offered himself in his place?

   _____

   _____

   _____

   _____

   _____

3. What do you think Joseph was up to by demanding the brothers bring Benjamin with them if they came back and making it look as if Benjamin had stolen from him? What was he trying to accomplish?

_____

_____

_____

_____

_____

_____

4. Why do you think the brothers were terrified of Joseph when he revealed his identity?

_____

_____

_____

_____

_____

❷ Joshua Has to Make a Choice

Joshua 9:1–27

¹ Now when all the kings west of the Jordan heard about these things—the kings in the hill country, in the western foothills, and along the entire coast of the Mediterranean Sea as far as Lebanon (the kings of the Hittites, Amorites, Canaanites, Perizzites, Hivites and Jebusites)— ² they came together to wage war against Joshua and Israel.

³ However, when the people of Gibeon heard what Joshua had done to Jericho and Ai, ⁴ they resorted to a ruse: They went as a delegation whose donkeys were loaded with worn-out sacks and old wineskins, cracked and mended. ⁵ They put worn and patched sandals on their feet and wore old clothes. All the bread of their food supply was dry and moldy. ⁶ Then they went to Joshua in the camp at Gilgal and said to him and the Israelites, "We have come from a distant country; make a treaty with us."

7 The Israelites said to the Hivites, "But perhaps you live near us, so how can we make a treaty with you?"

8 "We are your servants," they said to Joshua.

But Joshua asked, "Who are you and where do you come from?"

9 They answered: "Your servants have come from a very distant country because of the fame of the Lord your God. For we have heard reports of him: all that he did in Egypt, 10 and all that he did to the two kings of the Amorites east of the Jordan—Sihon king of Heshbon, and Og king of Bashan, who reigned in Ashtaroth.11 And our elders and all those living in our country said to us, 'Take provisions for your journey; go and meet them and say to them, "We are your servants; make a treaty with us."' 12 This bread of ours was warm when we packed it at home on the day we left to come to you. But now see how dry and moldy it is. 13 And these wineskins that we filled were new, but see how cracked they are. And our clothes and sandals are worn out by the very long journey."

14 The Israelites sampled their provisions but did not inquire of the Lord. 15 Then Joshua made a treaty of peace with them to let them live, and the leaders of the assembly ratified it by oath.

16 Three days after they made the treaty with the Gibeonites, the Israelites heard that they were neighbors, living near them. 17 So the Israelites set out and on the third day came to their cities: Gibeon, Kephirah, Beeroth and Kiriath Jearim. 18 But the Israelites did not attack them, because the leaders of the assembly had sworn an oath to them by the Lord, the God of Israel.

The whole assembly grumbled against the leaders, 19 but all the leaders answered, "We have given them our oath by the Lord, the God of Israel, and we cannot touch them now. 20 This is what we will do to them: We will let them live, so that God's wrath will not fall on us for breaking the oath we swore to them."

21 They continued, "Let them live, but let them be woodcutters and water carriers in the service of the whole assembly." So the leaders' promise to them was kept.

22 Then Joshua summoned the Gibeonites and said, "Why did you deceive us by saying, 'We live a long way from you,' while actually you live near us? 23 You are now under a curse: You will never be released from service as woodcutters and water carriers for the house of my God."

24 They answered Joshua, "Your servants were clearly told how the Lord your God had commanded his servant Moses to give you the whole land and to wipe out all its inhabitants from before you. So we feared for our lives because of you, and that is why we did this. ²⁵ We are now in your hands. Do to us whatever seems good and right to you."

²⁶ So Joshua saved them from the Israelites, and they did not kill them. ²⁷ That day he made the Gibeonites woodcutters and water carriers for the assembly, to provide for the needs of the altar of the LORD at the place the LORD would choose. And that is what they are to this day.

Joshua 10:1–11

¹ Now Adoni-Zedek king of Jerusalem heard that Joshua had taken Ai and totally destroyed it, doing to Ai and its king as he had done to Jericho and its king, and that the people of Gibeon had made a treaty of peace with Israel and had become their allies. ² He and his people were very much alarmed at this, because Gibeon was an important city, like one of the royal cities; it was larger than Ai, and all its men were good fighters. ³ So Adoni-Zedek king of Jerusalem appealed to Hoham king of Hebron, Piram king of Jarmuth, Japhia king of Lachish and Debir king of Eglon. ⁴ "Come up and help me attack Gibeon," he said, "because it has made peace with Joshua and the Israelites."

⁵ Then the five kings of the Amorites—the kings of Jerusalem, Hebron, Jarmuth, Lachish and Eglon—joined forces. They moved up with all their troops and took up positions against Gibeon and attacked it.

⁶ The Gibeonites then sent word to Joshua in the camp at Gilgal: "Do not abandon your servants. Come up to us quickly and save us! Help us, because all the Amorite kings from the hill country have joined forces against us."

⁷ So Joshua marched up from Gilgal with his entire army, including all the best fighting men. ⁸ The LORD said to Joshua, "Do not be afraid of them; I have given them into your hand. Not one of them will be able to withstand you."

⁹ After an all-night march from Gilgal, Joshua took them by surprise. ¹⁰ The LORD threw them into confusion before Israel, so Joshua and the Israelites defeated them completely at Gibeon. Israel pursued them along the road going up to Beth Horon and cut them down all the way to Azekah and Makkedah. ¹¹ As they fled before Israel on the road down from Beth Horon to Azekah, the LORD hurled large hailstones down on them, and more of them died from the hail than were killed by the swords of the Israelites.

Study Questions

1. The children of Israel had been told by God repeatedly not to make treaties with any of the people who lived in the promised land they were entering (Exodus 34:12; Deuteronomy 7:2), yet that's what they ended up doing with the Gibeonites. Where did Joshua and the Israelites go wrong?

   _____

   _____

   _____

   _____

   _____

2. When Joshua and the Israelites found out the people of Gibeon lived close by and had deceived them, most of the Israelites want to kill them. Would they have been justified? Whose reaction was right: the people who wanted to kill them or the leaders who wanted to honor their oath? Explain.

   _____

   _____

   _____

   _____

   _____

   _____

3. The passage says Joshua "made a treaty of peace with them to let them live." It does not mention any obligation to protect or fight for the Gibeonites, yet that is what Joshua did. Was Joshua simply maintaining his integrity, or was he going above and beyond it? Explain. What was the result of his actions?

   _____

   _____

   _____

   _____

   _____

   _____

❸ Weigh Your Words and Your Promises

Ecclesiastes 5:1–7

¹ Guard your steps when you go to the house of God. Go near to listen rather than to offer the sacrifice of fools, who do not know that they do wrong.

> *² Do not be quick with your mouth,*
>> *do not be hasty in your heart*
>> *to utter anything before God.*
> *God is in heaven*
>> *and you are on earth,*
>> *so let your words be few.*
> *³ A dream comes when there are many cares,*
>> *and many words mark the speech of a fool.*

⁴ When you make a vow to God, do not delay to fulfill it. He has no pleasure in fools; fulfill your vow. ⁵ It is better not to make a vow than to make one and not fulfill it. ⁶ Do not let your mouth lead you into sin. And do not protest to the temple messenger, "My vow was a mistake." Why should God be angry at what you say and destroy the work of your hands?⁷ Much dreaming and many words are meaningless. Therefore fear God.

Study Questions

1. The context of this passage relates to our interaction with God. How much of its instruction also applies to our interaction with people?

   _____

   _____

   _____

   _____

   _____

   _____

   _____

   _____

2. What lessons can you find in this passage on communication, decision making, and leadership?

_____

_____

_____

_____

3. The writer of Ecclesiastes uses the word *fool* several times in this passage. What are the characteristics of a fool, and how do they differ from a person of integrity?

_____

_____

_____

_____

LEADERSHIP INSIGHT AND REFLECTION

What values did the various leaders in these passages display? Write the names of the people along with their values.

_____

_____

_____

_____

_____

_____

What values are important for you as a person and leader? Make a list and include a sentence or phrase with each describing why it's important to you.

_____

_____

_____

_____

_____

_____

Rate yourself on how consistently you are living out each value from best to worst. Write a 1 next to the value you live out most consistently, a 2 next to the one you live out next best, and so on until you've placed a number by each. Which was your worst?

_____
_____
_____
_____

How is your worst area impacting your soul, your relationships, and your leadership? Take some time to do honest assessment and write your answers here.

_____
_____
_____
_____
_____
_____

Taking Action

How does God want you to improve and change, especially in your weakest area, so that you can improve your integrity?

_____
_____
_____
_____
_____

What positive tangible step do you need to take? When will you take it, and what will you do to remain consistent in that area day to day in the future?

_____
_____
_____
_____
_____

Group Discussion Questions

1. Joseph was sold into slavery by his brothers because he was his father's favorite. After Israel believed Joseph was dead, he doted on Joseph's full brother Benjamin. Why do you think Judah stood up for Benjamin and offered to become a slave in his place these many years later? What had changed?

2. After revealing himself, Joseph showed his brothers mercy, even though he had the power to punish them in any way he desired. What does that say about Joseph's integrity?

3. Why do you think the reaction of Joshua and the leaders to the Gibeonites' deception was different from the reaction of all the other Israelites?

4. How would you have responded if you had been in Joshua's place and found out the delegation from Gibeon had lied to you and caused you to violate God's command not to make a treaty with people in the promised land or to show them mercy?

5. What insight have you gained about making and keeping promises based on the Ecclesiastes passage?

6. What was your greatest takeaway about integrity and how it effects leadership based on this lesson?

7. What action do you believe God is asking you to take to grow in integrity as a result of this lesson? When will you do it and how will you consistently follow through?

LESSON 5

FOLLOWERSHIP

Good Leaders Are Great Followers First

THE ISSUE DEFINED

There is a common misconception about leading and following. It assumes that every individual falls into either the "leader" or "follower" category. But it's not either-or. It's both all the time. Nobody only follows or only leads. Instead, followership is an interplay that leaders must navigate from moment to moment. In many situations, leaders do take the lead. They cast vision and set direction for their organization. But they must also be willing to follow when deferring to the expertise of others on the team or to their own leaders.

Watch the interplay of people during a meeting. In a healthy environment, different people take the lead based on the situation and the skills needed in the moment. Egotistical leaders believe they must lead in any and every situation. But wise leaders listen and give time to everyone who has something to contribute.

A problem often arises when a person in a position of leadership has never actually learned to follow well. Without experience in followership, they don't have a good frame of reference for what it feels like to be led. They don't understand the effort it takes to learn to yield to someone else's authority. And this lack of experience actually makes them insecure as leaders. So they tend to avoid interactions where they might need to listen to their people or change a decision based on the input of others. They act like the kind of leader that they themselves would hate to follow—a dictator.

Bishop Fulton J. Sheen remarked, "Civilization is always in danger when those who have never learned to obey are given the right to command." Only a leader who has followed well knows how to lead others well. Good leadership requires an understanding of the world that followers live in. The best leaders are able to connect with their people because they have walked in their shoes. Because they know what it means to be under authority, they have a better sense of how authority should be exercised.

Leaders who know how to follow tend to be more flexible, realistic, grateful, and respectful of their followers' time and effort. In contrast, leaders who have never followed well or submitted to authority tend to be prideful, unrealistic, rigid, and autocratic. These arrogant leaders are rarely effective in the long run. They alienate their followers, their colleagues, and their leaders.

Before we will ever become leaders of integrity, we must learn to follow others with integrity. In fact, the acid test of character comes when we disagree with people who possess legitimate authority. When we refuse to demand our own way and instead submit to others for the benefit of the team or organization, our hearts are right. This is when God can trust us to lead others.

CASE STUDIES

Read these case studies from the Bible and answer the study questions that follow.

① Daniel Finds a Way to Follow While Maintaining His Values

Daniel 1:1–21

¹ In the third year of the reign of Jehoiakim king of Judah, Nebuchadnezzar king of Babylon came to Jerusalem and besieged it. ² And the Lord delivered Jehoiakim king of Judah into his hand, along with some of the articles from the temple of God. These he carried off to the temple of his god in Babylonia and put in the treasure house of his god.

³ Then the king ordered Ashpenaz, chief of his court officials, to bring into the king's service some of the Israelites from the royal family and the nobility— ⁴ young men without any physical defect, handsome, showing aptitude for every kind of learning, well informed, quick to understand, and qualified to serve in the king's palace. He was to teach them the language and literature of the Babylonians. ⁵ The king assigned them a daily amount of food and wine from the king's table. They were to be trained for three years, and after that they were to enter the king's service.

⁶ Among those who were chosen were some from Judah: Daniel, Hananiah, Mishael and Azariah. ⁷ The chief official gave them new names: to Daniel, the name Belteshazzar; to Hananiah, Shadrach; to Mishael, Meshach; and to Azariah, Abednego.

⁸ But Daniel resolved not to defile himself with the royal food and wine, and he asked the chief official for permission not to defile himself this way. ⁹ Now God had caused the official to show favor and compassion to Daniel, ¹⁰ but the official told Daniel, "I am afraid of my lord the king, who has assigned your food and drink. Why should he see you looking worse than the other young men your age? The king would then have my head because of you."

¹¹ Daniel then said to the guard whom the chief official had appointed over Daniel, Hananiah, Mishael and Azariah, ¹² "Please test your servants for ten days: Give us nothing but vegetables to eat and water to drink. ¹³ Then compare our appearance with that of the young men who eat the royal food, and treat your servants in accordance with what you see." ¹⁴ So he agreed to this and tested them for ten days.

¹⁵ At the end of the ten days they looked healthier and better nourished than any of the young men who ate the royal food. ¹⁶ So the guard took away their choice food and the wine they were to drink and gave them vegetables instead.

¹⁷ To these four young men God gave knowledge and understanding of all kinds of literature and learning. And Daniel could understand visions and dreams of all kinds.

¹⁸ At the end of the time set by the king to bring them into his service, the chief official presented them to Nebuchadnezzar. ¹⁹ The king talked with them, and he found none equal to Daniel, Hananiah, Mishael and Azariah; so they entered the king's service. ²⁰ In every matter of wisdom and understanding about which the king questioned them, he found them ten times better than all the magicians and enchanters in his whole kingdom.

²¹ And Daniel remained there until the first year of King Cyrus.

Study Questions

1. Before he was taken away from Jerusalem by King Nebuchadnezzar, Daniel must have been a member of the nobility or the royal family. How do you think he felt being an exile in Babylon?

   _____

   _____

   _____

   _____

2. Daniel believed eating food from the king's table was wrong, yet he desired to submit to authority. How did he resolve this conflict? How well did it work?

   _____

   _____

   _____

   _____

3. What do you think Daniel would have done if the chief official had ordered him to eat from the king's table? Do you believe it would have changed the outcome for Daniel and the others? Explain.

   _____

   _____

   _____

   _____

4. It's believed that Daniel served in Babylon from 605 BC to 539 BC, which was the first year of King Cyrus's reign, and even became the ruler of the province of Babylon (see Daniel 2:48). What does this say about the leadership potential of those who follow well and do it with excellence?

   _____

   _____

   _____

   _____

   _____

② Authority and the Chain of Command

Luke 7:1–10

¹ When Jesus had finished saying all this to the people who were listening, he entered Capernaum. ² There a centurion's servant, whom his master valued highly, was sick and about to die. ³ The centurion heard of Jesus and sent some elders of the Jews to him, asking him to come and heal his servant. ⁴ When they came to Jesus, they pleaded earnestly with him, "This man deserves to have you do this,⁵ because he loves our nation and has built our synagogue." ⁶ So Jesus went with them.

He was not far from the house when the centurion sent friends to say to him: "Lord, don't trouble yourself, for I do not deserve to have you come under my roof.⁷ That is why I did not even consider myself worthy to come to you. But say the word, and my servant will be healed. ⁸ For I myself am a man under authority, with soldiers under me. I tell this one, 'Go,' and he goes; and that one, 'Come,' and he comes. I say to my servant, 'Do this,' and he does it."

⁹ When Jesus heard this, he was amazed at him, and turning to the crowd following him, he said, "I tell you, I have not found such great faith even in Israel."¹⁰ Then the men who had been sent returned to the house and found the servant well.

Study Questions

1. The centurion describes how people under his command respond to him, but he also describes himself as a man under authority. What does that mean? How would that impact his choices and behavior?

   _____

   _____

   _____

   _____

   _____

   _____

   _____

2. When the centurion says, "Say the word , and my servant will be healed," what kind of authority is he saying that Jesus has?

_____

_____

_____

_____

3. Jesus was amazed by the centurion's faith. How was their interaction an issue of faith?

_____

_____

_____

_____

4. How was their interaction an issue of leadership and followership?

_____

_____

_____

_____

❸ Submission to Governing Authorities

Romans 13:1–7

¹ Let everyone be subject to the governing authorities, for there is no authority except that which God has established. The authorities that exist have been established by God. ² Consequently, whoever rebels against the authority is rebelling against what God has instituted, and those who do so will bring judgment on themselves. ³ For rulers hold no terror for those who do right, but for those who do wrong. Do you want to be free from fear of the one in authority? Then do what is right and you will be commended. ⁴ For the one in authority is God's servant for your good. But if you do wrong, be afraid, for rulers do not bear the sword for no reason. They are God's servants, agents of wrath to bring punishment on the wrongdoer. ⁵ Therefore, it is necessary to

*submit to the authorities, not only because of possible punishment but also
as a matter of conscience.*

*6 This is also why you pay taxes, for the authorities are God's servants, who
give their full time to governing. 7 Give to everyone what you owe them: If you
owe taxes, pay taxes; if revenue, then revenue; if respect, then respect; if honor,
then honor.*

Study Questions

1. What is your response to Paul's statement that there is no authority except
   that which God has established? How readily do you accept it? How do you
   react emotionally? How do you reconcile it in light of oppressive leaders?

   _____

   _____

   _____

   _____

   _____

2. Paul says that governing authorities are God's servants for your good, but he
   also describes them as agents of wrath to bring punishment on the wrongdoer. How can both of those things be true at the same time? In light of this,
   how does followership require trust in God?

   _____

   _____

   _____

   _____

3. How do you think submission to authority and followership is a "matter of
   conscience" as Paul describes? What impact does refusing to submit have
   on the follower? On the leader? On the greater good?

   _____

   _____

   _____

   _____

   _____

4. Paul says, "Give to everyone what you owe them." How do you determine what you owe? What role, if any, do justice and fairness have in this aspect of followership?

_____

_____

_____

_____

_____

Leadership Insight and Reflection

Think about the dynamics at work in each of the passages you read. Daniel was ordered to become a servant in a foreign land after being involuntarily exiled from his home. Jesus was asked to heal the servant of a Roman centurion whose government had conquered his land and oppressed his people. Paul admonished people to obey that same government which had conquered most of the western world and taxed its people. Why would all of these leaders support the concept of followership?

_____

_____

_____

_____

_____

_____

_____

How do you decide when it's good and right to submit to authority and follow, and when it's right and appropriate not to follow?

_____

_____

_____

_____

_____

_____

_____

Which is the greater issue for you personally? Do you have a difficult time following authority when you should? Or do you have a more difficult time standing up when you should? Why? Explain.

_____

_____

_____

_____

_____

_____

How would growing in the area of followership make you a better team member? How would it make you a better leader?

_____

_____

_____

_____

_____

_____

TAKING ACTION

What change in attitude or action must you take to grow in followership?

_____

_____

_____

_____

_____

What will you commit to do? When and how will you do it?

_____

_____

_____

_____

_____

GROUP DISCUSSION QUESTIONS

1. What is your gut reaction to the word *followership*? Is it positive or negative? Explain.

2. If you had been in Daniel's place, would you have eaten the food provided, tried to work around the problem in secret, or asked permission to do something different the way Daniel did? Explain your answer.

3. What does your answer to the previous question say about your mindset regarding authority?

4. The Luke passage says the elders of the Jews went to Jesus at the centurion's request to ask Jesus to heal the sick servant. What does the elders' actions say about their followership? Whose authority were they acknowledging by making their request?

5. What is your natural response to Paul's words, "If you owe taxes, pay taxes; if revenue, then revenue; if respect, then respect; if honor, then honor"? Which do you find the most difficult to give?

6. What was your greatest takeaway about followership from this lesson?

7. What action do you believe God is asking you to take in followership to make you a better leader? When and how will you take it?

LESSON 6

SELF-LEADERSHIP

Everything Worthwhile Is Uphill

THE ISSUE DEFINED

As leaders, one of our greatest struggles is leading ourselves first. Many highly gifted people have stopped far short of their leadership potential because they were not willing to pay this price. They tried to take the fast track to leadership only to find that shortcuts never pay off in the long run. We can't expect to take others farther than we have gone ourselves.

A truth that we need to recognize, not just for leadership but for all of life, is that everything worthwhile is uphill all the way. The word *everything* is inclusive. It's all-encompassing. Pair that with *worthwhile*—the things that are desirable, appropriate, good for you, attractive, beneficial. It's all *uphill*, meaning the pursuit of it is challenging, grueling, exhausting, strenuous, and difficult. And it's *all the way*. Why is that significant? Anyone can climb for a short time. Nearly everyone does—at least once. But can you sustain it? Can you climb every day, day after day, year after year? Can you keep leading yourself well?

There is no such thing as accidental achievement. Any climb uphill must be deliberate, consistent, and willful. It is an intentional choice, internally motivated. That requires self-leadership. The leader who learns self-leadership moves from good intentions to good actions. That is what separates words and ideas from actual results. One of the greatest gaps in life is between sounding good and doing good. We are ultimately measured by what we do and how our actions shape the world around us.

There are two types of people in the area of self-leadership. One type puts off what needs to be done and plays now, preferring to avoid doing what he or she must. The other type pays now by doing the necessary, even if it's unpleasant, and is willing to defer fun and play later. The thing you need to know is that everybody pays. Whatever you put off until later, compounds. If you put off playing, you get to play more later. If you put off paying, you have to pay more later. There is no cheating life.

If you only do what you want to do, you will never get to do what you *really* want to do. Self-leadership is developed by saying yes when we want to say no and saying no when we want to say yes. There are two types of pain in life. The pain of doing hard things, which is enabled with self-leadership, and the pain of regret, which aches until we die.

CASE STUDIES

Read these case studies from the Bible and answer the study questions that follow.

① A Noble Example of a Good Self-Leadership

Proverbs 31:10–31

¹⁰ *A wife of noble character who can find?*
      She is worth far more than rubies.
¹¹ *Her husband has full confidence in her*
      and lacks nothing of value.
¹² *She brings him good, not harm,*
      all the days of her life.
¹³ *She selects wool and flax*
      and works with eager hands.
¹⁴ *She is like the merchant ships,*
      bringing her food from afar.

¹⁵ *She gets up while it is still night;*
  she provides food for her family
  and portions for her female servants.
¹⁶ *She considers a field and buys it;*
  out of her earnings she plants a vineyard.
¹⁷ *She sets about her work vigorously;*
  her arms are strong for her tasks.
¹⁸ *She sees that her trading is profitable,*
  and her lamp does not go out at night.
¹⁹ *In her hand she holds the distaff*
  and grasps the spindle with her fingers.
²⁰ *She opens her arms to the poor*
  and extends her hands to the needy.
²¹ *When it snows, she has no fear for her household;*
  for all of them are clothed in scarlet.
²² *She makes coverings for her bed;*
  she is clothed in fine linen and purple.
²³ *Her husband is respected at the city gate,*
  where he takes his seat among the elders of the land.
²⁴ *She makes linen garments and sells them,*
  and supplies the merchants with sashes.
²⁵ *She is clothed with strength and dignity;*
  she can laugh at the days to come.
²⁶ *She speaks with wisdom,*
  and faithful instruction is on her tongue.
²⁷ *She watches over the affairs of her household*
  and does not eat the bread of idleness.
²⁸ *Her children arise and call her blessed;*
  her husband also, and he praises her:
²⁹ *"Many women do noble things,*
  but you surpass them all."
³⁰ *Charm is deceptive, and beauty is fleeting;*
  but a woman who fears the LORD is to be praised.
³¹ *Honor her for all that her hands have done,*
  and let her works bring her praise at the city gate.

Study Questions

1. What examples of good self-leadership can you find in this descriptive passage? List as many of them as you can find.

2. What are the motivations of this leader?

3. How much of what she does depends on good choices? How much on thinking ahead? How much on wisdom? How much on experience? Describe how you think those factors interplay when it comes to good self-leadership.

4. What impact does this leader have on her "team"? What impact does she have in the community?

_____

_____

_____

_____

_____

_____

2 Invite the Holy Spirit to Help with Self-Leadership

Galatians 5:13–26

13 You, my brothers and sisters, were called to be free. But do not use your freedom to indulge the flesh; rather, serve one another humbly in love. 14 For the entire law is fulfilled in keeping this one command: "Love your neighbor as yourself." 15 If you bite and devour each other, watch out or you will be destroyed by each other.

16 So I say, walk by the Spirit, and you will not gratify the desires of the flesh. 17 For the flesh desires what is contrary to the Spirit, and the Spirit what is contrary to the flesh. They are in conflict with each other, so that you are not to do whatever you want. 18 But if you are led by the Spirit, you are not under the law.

19 The acts of the flesh are obvious: sexual immorality, impurity and debauchery; 20 idolatry and witchcraft; hatred, discord, jealousy, fits of rage, selfish ambition, dissensions, factions 21 and envy; drunkenness, orgies, and the like. I warn you, as I did before, that those who live like this will not inherit the kingdom of God.

22 But the fruit of the Spirit is love, joy, peace, forbearance, kindness, goodness, faithfulness, 23 gentleness and self-control. Against such things there is no law. 24 Those who belong to Christ Jesus have crucified the flesh with its passions and desires. 25 Since we live by the Spirit, let us keep in step with the Spirit. 26 Let us not become conceited, provoking and envying each other.

Study Questions

1. In this letter, Paul admonishes his readers not to use the freedom they have to indulge themselves. How can this instruction be applied to leaders and leadership? Why does Paul offer humble service as the alternative? How are indulgence and service opposites?

   _____

   _____

   _____

   _____

   _____

   _____

2. Paul acknowledges Christians possess the desire to do what they want, and he follows it up with a long list of negative acts of the flesh. What temptations do you face when you hold a leadership position or possess power?

   _____

   _____

   _____

   _____

   _____

   _____

3. This passage lists the fruit of the Spirit. Paul's use of the word *fruit* implies that a process has already occurred: growth, flowering, and development. What spiritual process can you engage in to develop the fruit of the Spirit, so that you become a better person and leader?

   _____

   _____

   _____

   _____

   _____

   _____

4. It's implied in the passage that those who do not live by the Spirit are subject to conceit and are likely to provoke and envy others. How does this often play out with leaders?

_____

_____

_____

_____

_____

_____

❸ Paul Instructs Titus on Training in Self-Leadership

Titus 2:1–15

¹ You, however, must teach what is appropriate to sound doctrine. ² Teach the older men to be temperate, worthy of respect, self-controlled, and sound in faith, in love and in endurance.

³ Likewise, teach the older women to be reverent in the way they live, not to be slanderers or addicted to much wine, but to teach what is good. ⁴ Then they can urge the younger women to love their husbands and children, ⁵ to be self-controlled and pure, to be busy at home, to be kind, and to be subject to their husbands, so that no one will malign the word of God.

⁶ Similarly, encourage the young men to be self-controlled.
⁷ In everything set them an example by doing what is good. In your teaching show integrity, seriousness ⁸ and soundness of speech that cannot be condemned, so that those who oppose you may be ashamed because they have nothing bad to say about us.

⁹ Teach slaves to be subject to their masters in everything, to try to please them, not to talk back to them, ¹⁰ and not to steal from them, but to show that they can be fully trusted, so that in every way they will make the teaching about God our Savior attractive.

¹¹ For the grace of God has appeared that offers salvation to all people. ¹² It teaches us to say "No" to ungodliness and worldly passions, and to live self-controlled, upright and godly lives in this present age, ¹³ while we wait for the blessed hope—the appearing of the glory of our great God and Savior, Jesus Christ, ¹⁴ *who gave himself for us to redeem us from all wickedness and to purify for himself a people that are his very own, eager to do what is good.*

¹⁵ *These, then, are the things you should teach. Encourage and rebuke with all authority. Do not let anyone despise you.*

Study Questions

1. What characteristics of self-leadership does Paul cite in this letter to Titus?

2. What reason does he give for living the way he suggests? How does that apply to you? How does it help you to become a better leader?

3. Paul mentions the grace of God in this passage and says it helps us to live self-controlled lives. How do you think grace can help us?

4. Titus is told to teach these things to others and to encourage and rebuke them. How can a leader do this in a way that actually works and doesn't alienate people?

_____

_____

_____

_____

_____

_____

_____

_____

LEADERSHIP INSIGHT AND REFLECTION

The first passage from Proverbs describes a good leader working primarily in the home with her family. The passage from Galatians is directed to a general audience of believers. The letter to Titus is specific instruction to an appointed leader. What do they have in common?

_____

_____

_____

_____

_____

_____

_____

_____

_____

_____

_____

_____

_____

_____

Based on what you've learned from these passages, write a statement or philosophy of self-leadership for yourself.

_____
_____
_____
_____
_____
_____
_____
_____
_____
_____
_____

TAKING ACTION

Based on your statement of self-leadership, where are you currently falling short? Why are you falling short?

_____
_____
_____
_____
_____
_____
_____

What action can you take to improve your self-leadership immediately?

_____
_____
_____
_____
_____
_____
_____
_____
_____

How will you implement it?

_____

_____

_____

_____

_____

_____

_____

_____

_____

_____

_____

_____

_____

_____

GROUP DISCUSSION QUESTIONS

1. Do you think the description of the wife of noble character is a blueprint for model conduct or an idealized description that would be impossible for anyone to live up to? Explain.

2. Reread the acts of the flesh listed in Galatians 5:19–21. Which are driven physically? Which emotionally? Which intellectually? How and why do you think people are tempted in these areas?

3. What do you do to encourage the Spirit's work within you so that you exhibit the fruit of the Spirit?

4. In what areas of your life do you find the fight for self-leadership to be most difficult? Why?

5. According to the passage in Titus, how important is modeling self-leadership? How important is it according to the other two passages? Why does it matter? What is its value?

6. What is the impact of working with a team member who practices poor self-leadership? What is the impact of a leader who lacks good self-leadership? If you've worked with such a leader, describe what happened.

7. What action do you believe God is asking you to take to improve your own self-leadership? What will you do, and when will you do it?

LESSON 7

GROWTH

Tomorrow Gets Better
When You Get Better Today

THE ISSUE DEFINED

Your capacity to grow will ultimately determine your capacity to lead. Growth matters. If you try to lead out of what you learned long in the past, and you're not growing in the present, the clock is ticking on your time as a leader. Development, expansion, and the future of your leadership depend on your dedication to personal growth.

There are many reasons to pursue personal growth. It opens doors. It makes us better. It helps us achieve our career goals. Over time, it creates momentum in our lives. That in turn encourages us to grow even more. We start to place a greater emphasis on growing rather than on arriving, and that makes it easier for us to learn from our failure. But all of those things pale before the most important reason to pursue growth, because this reason has the greatest power to change our lives in every way. Personal growth increases hope. It teaches us tomorrow can be better than today.

Choosing to grow is the seed of hope. When leaders make growth a habit, they strengthen that hope. Growth over time realizes hope. When we take small steps of growth every day, over time, we see progress. String together enough days of consistent growth and you begin to change as a person. You become better, stronger, more skilled, or all of the above. And when you change yourself, you can change your circumstances. This begins a positive cycle of your growth strengthening your hope, and your hope strengthening your growth. When you do this week after week, month after month, year after year, you gradually move from hope imagined to hope realized.

One of the greatest enemies to growth is resistance to change. But growth equals change. Without a willingness to change, no one can improve or grow. The cost of change is often the great separator between those who grow and those who do not, between those who grow into their dreams, and those who dream but remain where they are.

To be realistic about any growth plan, wise leaders ask themselves: Am I willing to pay the price for my dream? The price of change usually comes sooner than you think, it's higher than you imagined it would be, and it must be paid more often than you expected. In fact, to continue growing is to continue paying the price of that growth.

Life begins at the end of our comfort zone. In order to grow, leaders must embrace change and learn to become comfortable being uncomfortable. People get stuck because they are unwilling to leave what they have known in order to do something better. If you want to grow as a person and as a leader, you must be willing to surrender feeling right so that you can find what actually is right. It doesn't require you to be brilliant, talented, or lucky. It just means you have to be willing to change and be uncomfortable.

CASE STUDIES

Read these case studies from the Bible and answer the study questions that follow.

① Go After Wisdom

Proverbs 4:1–27

¹ Listen, my sons, to a father's instruction;
    pay attention and gain understanding.
² I give you sound learning,
    so do not forsake my teaching.
³ For I too was a son to my father,
    still tender, and cherished by my mother.
⁴ Then he taught me, and he said to me,
    "Take hold of my words with all your heart;
    keep my commands, and you will live.
⁵ Get wisdom, get understanding;
    do not forget my words or turn away from them.

6 Do not forsake wisdom, and she will protect you;
  love her, and she will watch over you.
7 The beginning of wisdom is this: Get wisdom.
  Though it cost all you have, get understanding.
8 Cherish her, and she will exalt you;
  embrace her, and she will honor you.
9 She will give you a garland to grace your head
  and present you with a glorious crown."

10 Listen, my son, accept what I say,
  and the years of your life will be many.
11 I instruct you in the way of wisdom
  and lead you along straight paths.
12 When you walk, your steps will not be hampered;
  when you run, you will not stumble.
13 Hold on to instruction, do not let it go;
  guard it well, for it is your life.
14 Do not set foot on the path of the wicked
  or walk in the way of evildoers.
15 Avoid it, do not travel on it;
  turn from it and go on your way.
16 For they cannot rest until they do evil;
  they are robbed of sleep till they make someone stumble.
17 They eat the bread of wickedness
  and drink the wine of violence.

18 The path of the righteous is like the morning sun,
  shining ever brighter till the full light of day.
19 But the way of the wicked is like deep darkness;
  they do not know what makes them stumble.

20 My son, pay attention to what I say;
  turn your ear to my words.
21 Do not let them out of your sight,
  keep them within your heart;

*²² for they are life to those who find them
and health to one's whole body.*
*²³ Above all else, guard your heart,
for everything you do flows from it.*
*²⁴ Keep your mouth free of perversity;
keep corrupt talk far from your lips.*
*²⁵ Let your eyes look straight ahead;
fix your gaze directly before you.*
*²⁶ Give careful thought to the paths for your feet
and be steadfast in all your ways.*
*²⁷ Do not turn to the right or the left;
keep your foot from evil.*

Study Questions

1. What is the difference between wisdom and understanding? And what is the role of growth in acquiring them?

_____

_____

_____

_____

_____

_____

2. In what ways does the Proverbs writer say wisdom and understanding positively benefit a person? List as many as you can find in the passage.

_____

_____

_____

_____

_____

_____

_____

_____

_____

3. The Proverbs writer says that wisdom leads to righteousness and straight paths. What people does he write about in contrast to the wise? How are wisdom and wickedness opposites? Explain.

_____

_____

_____

_____

_____

_____

_____

_____

_____

_____

❷ Information Is Not Enough

Matthew 13:1–23

¹ That same day Jesus went out of the house and sat by the lake. ² Such large crowds gathered around him that he got into a boat and sat in it, while all the people stood on the shore. ³ Then he told them many things in parables, saying: "A farmer went out to sow his seed. ⁴ As he was scattering the seed, some fell along the path, and the birds came and ate it up. ⁵ Some fell on rocky places, where it did not have much soil. It sprang up quickly, because the soil was shallow. ⁶ But when the sun came up, the plants were scorched, and they withered because they had no root. ⁷ Other seed fell among thorns, which grew up and choked the plants. ⁸ Still other seed fell on good soil, where it produced a crop—a hundred, sixty or thirty times what was sown. ⁹ Whoever has ears, let them hear."

¹⁰ The disciples came to him and asked, "Why do you speak to the people in parables?"

¹¹ He replied, "Because the knowledge of the secrets of the kingdom of heaven has been given to you, but not to them. ¹² Whoever has will be given more, and they will have an abundance. Whoever does not have, even what they have will be taken from them. ¹³ This is why I speak to them in parables:

"Though seeing, they do not see;
    though hearing, they do not hear or understand.

¹⁴ In them is fulfilled the prophecy of Isaiah:

"'You will be ever hearing but never understanding;
    you will be ever seeing but never perceiving.
¹⁵ For this people's heart has become calloused;
    they hardly hear with their ears,
    and they have closed their eyes.
Otherwise they might see with their eyes,
    hear with their ears,
    understand with their hearts
and turn, and I would heal them.'"

¹⁶ But blessed are your eyes because they see, and your ears because they hear. ¹⁷ For truly I tell you, many prophets and righteous people longed to see what you see but did not see it, and to hear what you hear but did not hear it.

¹⁸ "Listen then to what the parable of the sower means: ¹⁹ When anyone hears the message about the kingdom and does not understand it, the evil one comes and snatches away what was sown in their heart. This is the seed sown along the path. ²⁰ The seed falling on rocky ground refers to someone who hears the word and at once receives it with joy. ²¹ But since they have no root, they last only a short time. When trouble or persecution comes because of the word, they quickly fall away. ²² The seed falling among the thorns refers to someone who hears the word, but the worries of this life and the deceitfulness of wealth choke the word, making it unfruitful. ²³ But the seed falling on good soil refers to someone who hears the word and understands it. This is the one who produces a crop, yielding a hundred, sixty or thirty times what was sown."

Study Questions

1. Jesus described the people who didn't understand his parables as seeing but not able to perceive and hearing without understanding. How does that concept apply to people who do not grow?

   _____

   _____

   _____

   _____

   _____

   _____

2. When Jesus spoke in parables, do you think he was trying to deliberately confuse certain people? Was he using it as a filter to separate people? Was he trying to make his teaching clear and timeless? What was his strategy? And what does it say about growth?

   _____

   _____

   _____

   _____

   _____

   _____

3. This parable from Matthew describes a spiritual process. It depicts reactions to the Word of God. However, it could also be applied to growth more generally. Taking your cue from Jesus's explanation, how would you interpret each of the soils in the context of personal growth?

   Rocky Soil:_____

   _____

   _____

   _____

   _____

Shallow Soil:_____

_____

_____

_____

_____

Thorny Soil:_____

_____

_____

_____

_____

Good Soil:_____

_____

_____

_____

_____

❸ Why We Must Keep Learning

Hebrews 5:11–14

[11] We have much to say about this, but it is hard to make it clear to you because you no longer try to understand. [12] In fact, though by this time you ought to be teachers, you need someone to teach you the elementary truths of God's word all over again. You need milk, not solid food! [13] Anyone who lives on milk, being still an infant, is not acquainted with the teaching about righteousness. [14] But solid food is for the mature, who by constant use have trained themselves to distinguish good from evil.

Hebrews 6:1–12

[1] Therefore let us move beyond the elementary teachings about Christ and be taken forward to maturity, not laying again the foundation of repentance

from acts that lead to death, and of faith in God, ² instruction about cleansing rites, the laying on of hands, the resurrection of the dead, and eternal judgment. ³ And God permitting, we will do so.

⁴ It is impossible for those who have once been enlightened, who have tasted the heavenly gift, who have shared in the Holy Spirit, ⁵ who have tasted the goodness of the word of God and the powers of the coming age ⁶ and who have fallen away, to be brought back to repentance. To their loss they are crucifying the Son of God all over again and subjecting him to public disgrace. ⁷ Land that drinks in the rain often falling on it and that produces a crop useful to those for whom it is farmed receives the blessing of God. ⁸ But land that produces thorns and thistles is worthless and is in danger of being cursed. In the end it will be burned.

⁹ Even though we speak like this, dear friends, we are convinced of better things in your case—the things that have to do with salvation. ¹⁰ God is not unjust; he will not forget your work and the love you have shown him as you have helped his people and continue to help them. ¹¹ We want each of you to show this same diligence to the very end, so that what you hope for may be fully realized. ¹² We do not want you to become lazy, but to imitate those who through faith and patience inherit what has been promised.

Study Questions

1. The Hebrews writer uses the phrase "you no longer try to understand" to describe the people he is addressing. What is he implying about them? What is their problem?

_____

_____

_____

_____

_____

_____

_____

_____

_____

2. What is the difference between milk and solid food? How is each consumed? What is required for milk versus solid food to be eaten? How does that metaphor relate to the idea of growth?

_____

_____

_____

_____

_____

_____

_____

3. The passage says that the people being addressed should be able to teach others at this point, but instead they need someone else to reteach them the basics. What are the leadership implications of this? How could the people solve this problem? How could they be sure it never occurs again?

_____

_____

_____

_____

_____

_____

_____

4. Look at the description of land in the passage. Why does the writer use that metaphor? How does the productivity of land correlate to growth? What can you learn from it?

_____

_____

_____

_____

_____

_____

_____

_____

LEADERSHIP INSIGHT AND REFLECTION

What are the connections between growth, understanding, wisdom, and productivity based on these three passages?

_____

_____

_____

_____

_____

_____

_____

_____

_____

_____

_____

_____

_____

Most of the teaching on growth in these passages is not specific to leadership, but you can draw conclusions about the importance of growth for good leadership. How are growth and leadership connected? What happens when leaders neglect their growth?

_____

_____

_____

_____

_____

_____

_____

_____

_____

_____

_____

_____

_____

How much of a priority has spiritual growth been to you in the past? How much of a priority has leadership growth been? What have been the results?

_____

_____

_____

_____

_____

_____

_____

_____

_____

_____

TAKING ACTION

In what area do you believe you should be growing to become a better leader? How would you like to grow? Be specific. How long do you think it will take? How would that growth benefit you? How would it benefit the people you lead?

_____

_____

_____

_____

_____

_____

_____

_____

_____

_____

_____

_____

_____

_____

What can you commit to do daily or weekly to follow through with that growth? When will you start?

_____

_____

_____

_____

_____

_____

_____

_____

_____

_____

_____

_____

_____

_____

_____

GROUP DISCUSSION QUESTIONS

1. What do you make of the statement, "The beginning of wisdom is this: Get wisdom," in Proverbs 4:7? Explain it in your own words.

2. The Proverbs passage focuses on the importance and benefits of acquiring wisdom and understanding and very little on the process. How do you think people should go about acquiring wisdom and understanding? What have you done in the past to acquire them?

3. When you look at your life spiritually, which of the four soils describes you: rocky, shallow, thorny, or good? Explain?

4. What about if you look at your leadership life? Which soil describes you and why?

5. Is it possible for people to be successful if they are productive in leadership but not spiritually? How about if they're spiritually productive but not in leadership? Explain.

6. What was your greatest takeaway about growth gained from the Hebrews passage?

7. In what area do you most want to grow, how will it benefit you and your team, and what is your plan for pursuing it?

LESSON 8

RELATIONSHIPS

Leadership Is Always a People Business

THE ISSUE DEFINED

One of the greatest mistakes leaders make is spending too much time in their offices and not enough time out among the people. Leaders are often agenda driven, task focused, and action oriented because they like to get things done. They hole up in their offices, rush to meetings, and ignore everyone they pass in the halls along the way. What a mistake! First and foremost, leadership is a people business. If you forget the people, you undermine your leadership and you run the risk of having it erode away. Then one day when you think you're leading, you'll turn around and discover that nobody is following, and you're only taking a walk.

Some leaders who ignore the relational aspect of leadership rely on their position instead. Others expect their own competence to do "all the talking" for them. True, good leaders are competent, but they are also intentionally connected to their people. They do this by slowing down. The higher a person rises in leadership, the faster life seems to move. But relational leaders move at the speed of their people. The best leaders aren't necessarily the first to cross the finish line; they are the first to bring their people across with them.

Relational leaders value their people. Everyone wants to know that their leader sees them as human beings, not just as workers who can get things done for the boss or the organization. When followers feel valued by their leaders, they are more willing to trust, listen, and participate in the vision for the team.

Relational leaders value what their people value. This starts by learning what that is. They try to get to know every member of their team, both professionally and personally. When leaders know and care about what matters to their people, they're able to connect with them where they are and give them what they need. And when people have what they need, they are more willing to give of themselves to help the team.

Relational leaders add value to their people. This is especially important for Christian leaders. Adding value is a by-product of selfless love, which is how God calls us to lead. When we put our people first, we show God's love to them. This serves as both an encouragement and an example. Leaders who add value also create a culture of adding value within the organization, and everyone benefits.

Leaders who focus on relationships still have a passion for vision and a love of action, but they devote the majority of their energy to people. Leaders who tend only to business often end up losing the people *and* the business. But leaders who tend to the people usually build up the people—and the business.

CASE STUDIES

Read these case studies from the Bible and answer the study questions that follow.

① Jacob Blesses His Grandsons

Genesis 48:1–22

¹ Some time later Joseph was told, "Your father is ill." So he took his two sons Manasseh and Ephraim along with him. ² When Jacob was told, "Your son Joseph has come to you," Israel rallied his strength and sat up on the bed.

³ Jacob said to Joseph, "God Almighty appeared to me at Luz in the land of Canaan, and there he blessed me ⁴ and said to me, 'I am going to make you fruitful and increase your numbers. I will make you a community of peoples, and I will give this land as an everlasting possession to your descendants after you.'

⁵ "Now then, your two sons born to you in Egypt before I came to you here will be reckoned as mine; Ephraim and Manasseh will be mine, just as Reuben and Simeon are mine. ⁶ Any children born to you after them will be yours;

in the territory they inherit they will be reckoned under the names of their brothers. ⁷ As I was returning from Paddan, to my sorrow Rachel died in the land of Canaan while we were still on the way, a little distance from Ephrath. So I buried her there beside the road to Ephrath" (that is, Bethlehem).

⁸ When Israel saw the sons of Joseph, he asked, "Who are these?"

⁹ "They are the sons God has given me here," Joseph said to his father.

Then Israel said, "Bring them to me so I may bless them."

¹⁰ Now Israel's eyes were failing because of old age, and he could hardly see. So Joseph brought his sons close to him, and his father kissed them and embraced them.

¹¹ Israel said to Joseph, "I never expected to see your face again, and now God has allowed me to see your children too."

¹² Then Joseph removed them from Israel's knees and bowed down with his face to the ground. ¹³ And Joseph took both of them, Ephraim on his right toward Israel's left hand and Manasseh on his left toward Israel's right hand, and brought them close to him. ¹⁴ But Israel reached out his right hand and put it on Ephraim's head, though he was the younger, and crossing his arms, he put his left hand on Manasseh's head, even though Manasseh was the firstborn.

¹⁵ Then he blessed Joseph and said,

"May the God before whom my fathers
    Abraham and Isaac walked faithfully,
the God who has been my shepherd
    all my life to this day,
¹⁶ the Angel who has delivered me from all harm
    —may he bless these boys.
May they be called by my name
    and the names of my fathers Abraham and Isaac,
and may they increase greatly
    on the earth."

¹⁷ When Joseph saw his father placing his right hand on Ephraim's head he was displeased; so he took hold of his father's hand to move it from Ephraim's head to Manasseh's head. ¹⁸ Joseph said to him, "No, my father, this one is the firstborn; put your right hand on his head."

¹⁹ But his father refused and said, "I know, my son, I know. He too will become a people, and he too will become great. Nevertheless, his younger brother will be greater than he, and his descendants will become a group of nations." ²⁰ He blessed them that day and said,

*"In your name will Israel pronounce this blessing:
    'May God make you like Ephraim and Manasseh.'"*

So he put Ephraim ahead of Manasseh.
²¹ Then Israel said to Joseph, "I am about to die, but God will be with you and take you back to the land of your fathers. ²² And to you I give one more ridge of land than to your brothers, the ridge I took from the Amorites with my sword and my bow."

Study Questions

1. Jacob, whom God renamed Israel, said he thought he would never see his son Joseph again because Joseph's brothers had sold him into slavery and told their father he was dead. But as a slave, Joseph rose up to become second in command of Egypt. Based on this passage, how would you describe the relationship between Jacob and Joseph?

   _____

   _____

   _____

   _____

   _____

2. What does Jacob's blessing of Joseph's two sons tell you about his relationship with God, his relationship with his sons, and his desires for his grandchildren?

   _____

   _____

   _____

   _____

3. What leadership lesson can you learn from Jacob's crossing of his hands to make the blessing specific to each boy instead of doing the blessing in the traditional way, which Joseph expected him to follow?

_____

_____

_____

_____

_____

4. Jacob's desire for Ephraim and Manasseh to be reckoned as his, just as his sons Reuben and Simeon were, became fulfilled when the Israelites entered the promised land and they were among the tribes given land, just as the descendants of Jacob's other sons were. How was this significant to the history of the nation of Israel?

_____

_____

_____

_____

_____

_____

❷ Paul Defines Love

1 Corinthians 13:1–13

¹ If I speak in the tongues of men or of angels, but do not have love, I am only a resounding gong or a clanging cymbal. ² If I have the gift of prophecy and can fathom all mysteries and all knowledge, and if I have a faith that can move mountains, but do not have love, I am nothing. ³ If I give all I possess to the poor and give over my body to hardship that I may boast, but do not have love, I gain nothing.

⁴ Love is patient, love is kind. It does not envy, it does not boast, it is not proud. ⁵ It does not dishonor others, it is not self-seeking, it is not easily angered, it keeps no record of wrongs. ⁶ Love does not delight in evil but rejoices with the truth. *7 It always protects, always trusts, always hopes, always perseveres.*

8 Love never fails. But where there are prophecies, they will cease; where there are tongues, they will be stilled; where there is knowledge, it will pass away. 9 For we know in part and we prophesy in part, 10 but when completeness comes, what is in part disappears. 11 When I was a child, I talked like a child, I thought like a child, I reasoned like a child. When I became a man, I put the ways of childhood behind me. 12 For now we see only a reflection as in a mirror; then we shall see face to face. Now I know in part; then I shall know fully, even as I am fully known.

13 And now these three remain: faith, hope and love. But the greatest of these is love.

Study Questions

1. In this passage, Paul provides a broad definition of love. How does what he says apply to leadership?

   _____

   _____

   _____

   _____

2. What positive qualities, actions, or abilities does Paul name that he says are inferior to love? What principle does this teach you about relationships?

   _____

   _____

   _____

   _____

3. Paul says that love keeps no record of wrongs. How can a leader honor this admonition and still lead effectively?

   _____

   _____

   _____

   _____

4. Knowing that love protects, trusts, hopes, and perseveres, how should that guide your leadership of others?

_____

_____

_____

_____

_____

③ John Encourages Love Over Hate

1 John 2:3–11

³ We know that we have come to know him if we keep his commands. ⁴ Whoever says, "I know him," but does not do what he commands is a liar, and the truth is not in that person. ⁵ But if anyone obeys his word, love for God is truly made complete in them. This is how we know we are in him: ⁶ Whoever claims to live in him must live as Jesus did.

⁷ Dear friends, I am not writing you a new command but an old one, which you have had since the beginning. This old command is the message you have heard. ⁸ Yet I am writing you a new command; its truth is seen in him and in you, because the darkness is passing and the true light is already shining.

⁹ Anyone who claims to be in the light but hates a brother or sister is still in the darkness. ¹⁰ Anyone who loves their brother and sister lives in the light, and there is nothing in them to make them stumble. ¹¹ But anyone who hates a brother or sister is in the darkness and walks around in the darkness. They do not know where they are going, because the darkness has blinded them.

1 John 4:7–21

⁷ Dear friends, let us love one another, for love comes from God. Everyone who loves has been born of God and knows God. ⁸ Whoever does not love does not know God, because God is love. ⁹ This is how God showed his love among us: He sent his one and only Son into the world that we might live through him. ¹⁰ This is love: not that we loved God, but that he loved us and sent his Son as an atoning sacrifice for our sins. *11* Dear friends, since God so loved us, we also ought to love one another. *12* No one has ever seen God; but if we love one another, God lives in us and his love is made complete in us.

13 This is how we know that we live in him and he in us: He has given us of his Spirit. *14* And we have seen and testify that the Father has sent his Son to be the Savior of the world. *15* If anyone acknowledges that Jesus is the Son of God, God lives in them and they in God. *16* And so we know and rely on the love God has for us.

God is love. Whoever lives in love lives in God, and God in them. *17* This is how love is made complete among us so that we will have confidence on the day of judgment: In this world we are like Jesus. *18* There is no fear in love. But perfect love drives out fear, because fear has to do with punishment. The one who fears is not made perfect in love.

19 We love because he first loved us. *20* Whoever claims to love God yet hates a brother or sister is a liar. For whoever does not love their brother and sister, whom they have seen, cannot love God, whom they have not seen. *21* And he has given us this command: Anyone who loves God must also love their brother and sister.

Study Questions

1. John says that we are to live according to Jesus's standard and that anyone who hates a brother or sister is in darkness and blind. How do you respond to this emotionally, intellectually, and spiritually?

   _____

   _____

   _____

   _____

2. According to John, why should we be capable of loving others?

   _____

   _____

   _____

   _____

   _____

3. John writes about fear in the context of love. Why would he do that? Why does he say that love drives out fear? What is the connection? And how might that apply to leadership?

_____

_____

_____

_____

_____

4. John say that anyone who says he loves God yet doesn't love his brothers and sisters is a liar. If you experience conflict with someone or someone harms you, how can you resolve the problem and still maintain this standard?

_____

_____

_____

_____

_____

LEADERSHIP INSIGHT AND REFLECTION

Do our obligations for how we treat other people and build relationships with them differ, depending on who's involved? Jacob was interacting with family members. Paul was addressing a general audience. John was talking about brothers and sisters in the faith.

_____

_____

_____

_____

_____

_____

_____

_____

_____

_____

Do relational standards change when someone is leading? Or when dealing with non-believers? Think about your answer in the context of John's statement: "Whoever claims to live in him must live as Jesus did."

_____

_____

_____

_____

_____

_____

_____

_____

_____

_____

_____

_____

With whom in your personal life and leadership activities are you falling short of God's standard for building relationships? Write the names of the people and list how you are falling short. What are you doing wrong or neglecting to do?

_____

_____

_____

_____

_____

_____

_____

_____

_____

_____

_____

_____

TAKING ACTION

For each person you listed above, write what action you must take to put the relationship on the right track according to God's standard.

_____
_____
_____
_____
_____
_____
_____
_____
_____
_____
_____
_____
_____
_____
_____
_____

Now number the relationships in order from most important on down. Starting with that most important relationship, plan to make the change or take the action you listed above. When will you address the first one?

_____
_____
_____
_____
_____
_____
_____
_____
_____
_____
_____
_____

GROUP DISCUSSION QUESTIONS

1. Joseph was undoubtedly pleased that his sons received his father Jacob's blessing, yet it wasn't given in the way Joseph expected or might have hoped. In what ways is this typical of how relationships usually go?

2. Paul said that if he was able to communicate truth and knowledge but did it without love, he was nothing and just making noise. What implications does this truth have for how someone should lead?

3. What is your reaction to Paul's statement that love is greater than faith or hope?

4. How can a leader go about upholding John's command to love others, while still doing what's best for the organization or team, and preserving his or her leadership credibility?

5. What was your greatest takeaway about relationships from this lesson?

6. What action do you believe God is asking you to take to grow in relationship-building in your personal life or in your leadership? What, when and how will you do it?

LESSON 9

MOTIVES

You Must Choose How You Will Use Your Leadership

THE ISSUE DEFINED

Someone once said, "People have two reasons for doing anything—a good reason and the real reason." If you desire to be a good leader, the good reason must be the same as the real reason. In other words, your motives matter.

Naturally gifted leaders have capabilities that they can easily use for personal advantage. They often see things before others do, and they often see more than others see. As a result, they can enjoy the advantages of using good timing and seeing the big picture. That puts them in a position to make the most of opportunities. The question is not whether leaders have an advantage over others because the answer to that question is yes. The question is whether the leader will use that advantage for personal gain or for the benefit of everyone on the team.

If you are a leader—or want to become one—you need to ask yourself why you want to lead. There is a big difference between people who want to lead because they are genuinely interested in others and desire to help them, and people who are in it for only themselves. People who lead for selfish reasons seek . . .

- **Power:** They love control and will continue to add value to themselves by reducing the value of others.

- **Position:** Titles are their ego food. They continually make sure that others feel their authority and are aware of their rights as a leader.
- **Money:** They will use people and sell themselves for financial gain.
- **Prestige:** They want to look good more than they want to be or do good.

Wise leaders make a habit of questioning their own motives on a regular basis. They constantly ask themselves whether they are being driven by any of the selfish desires listed above. And they remind themselves of the right motivation: a genuine desire for the benefit of others. This discipline keeps leaders' natural selfishness in check and purifies their motives on a day-to-day basis.

CASE STUDIES

Read these case studies from the Bible and answer the study questions that follow.

❶ God Questions Jonah's Motives

Jonah 3:1–10

¹ Then the word of the Lord came to Jonah a second time: ² "Go to the great city of Nineveh and proclaim to it the message I give you."

³ Jonah obeyed the word of the Lord and went to Nineveh. Now Nineveh was a very large city; it took three days to go through it. ⁴ Jonah began by going a day's journey into the city, proclaiming, "Forty more days and Nineveh will be overthrown." ⁵ The Ninevites believed God. A fast was proclaimed, and all of them, from the greatest to the least, put on sackcloth.

⁶ When Jonah's warning reached the king of Nineveh, he rose from his throne, took off his royal robes, covered himself with sackcloth and sat down in the dust. ⁷ This is the proclamation he issued in Nineveh:

"By the decree of the king and his nobles:
    Do not let people or animals, herds or flocks, taste anything;
    do not let them eat or drink. ⁸ But let people and animals be

covered with sackcloth. Let everyone call urgently on God. Let them give up their evil ways and their violence. ⁹ Who knows? God may yet relent and with compassion turn from his fierce anger so that we will not perish."

¹⁰ When God saw what they did and how they turned from their evil ways, he relented and did not bring on them the destruction he had threatened.

Jonah 4:1–11

¹ But to Jonah this seemed very wrong, and he became angry. ² He prayed to the Lᴏʀᴅ, "Isn't this what I said, Lᴏʀᴅ, when I was still at home? That is what I tried to forestall by fleeing to Tarshish. I knew that you are a gracious and compassionate God, slow to anger and abounding in love, a God who relents from sending calamity. ³ Now, Lᴏʀᴅ, take away my life, for it is better for me to die than to live."

⁴ But the Lᴏʀᴅ replied, "Is it right for you to be angry?"

⁵ Jonah had gone out and sat down at a place east of the city. There he made himself a shelter, sat in its shade and waited to see what would happen to the city. ⁶ Then the Lᴏʀᴅ God provided a leafy plant and made it grow up over Jonah to give shade for his head to ease his discomfort, and Jonah was very happy about the plant. ⁷ But at dawn the next day God provided a worm, which chewed the plant so that it withered. ⁸ When the sun rose, God provided a scorching east wind, and the sun blazed on Jonah's head so that he grew faint. He wanted to die, and said, "It would be better for me to die than to live."

⁹ But God said to Jonah, "Is it right for you to be angry about the plant?"

"It is," he said. "And I'm so angry I wish I were dead."

¹⁰ But the Lᴏʀᴅ said, "You have been concerned about this plant, though you did not tend it or make it grow. It sprang up overnight and died overnight. ¹¹ And should I not have concern for the great city of Nineveh, in which there are more than a hundred and twenty thousand people who cannot tell their right hand from their left—and also many animals?"

Study Questions

1. The first time God asked Jonah to go to Nineveh and preach, Jonah tried to flee from God on a ship, was cast into the sea during a storm, and was swallowed by a huge fish (Jonah 1–2). In this passage, God tells Jonah a second time to go to Nineveh, and Jonah obeys. Why do you think he chose to obey this time?

_____

_____

_____

_____

_____

2. Why didn't Jonah want to go to Nineveh? What does it say about him as a leader and person?

_____

_____

_____

_____

3. Why do you think God chose to grow the leafy plant to provide shade for Jonah and then let it be destroyed by a worm?

_____

_____

_____

_____

_____

❷ Motives Matter

Matthew 6:1–18

¹ "Be careful not to practice your righteousness in front of others to be seen by them. If you do, you will have no reward from your Father in heaven.

² *"So when you give to the needy, do not announce it with trumpets, as the hypocrites do in the synagogues and on the streets, to be honored by others. Truly I tell you, they have received their reward in full. ³ But when you give to the needy, do not let your left hand know what your right hand is doing, ⁴ so that your giving may be in secret. Then your Father, who sees what is done in secret, will reward you.*

⁵ *"And when you pray, do not be like the hypocrites, for they love to pray standing in the synagogues and on the street corners to be seen by others. Truly I tell you, they have received their reward in full. ⁶ But when you pray, go into your room, close the door and pray to your Father, who is unseen. Then your Father, who sees what is done in secret, will reward you. ⁷ And when you pray, do not keep on babbling like pagans, for they think they will be heard because of their many words. ⁸ Do not be like them, for your Father knows what you need before you ask him.*

⁹ *"This, then, is how you should pray:*

"'Our Father in heaven,
hallowed be your name,
¹⁰ *your kingdom come,*
your will be done,
        on earth as it is in heaven.
¹¹ *Give us today our daily bread.*
¹² *And forgive us our debts,*
        as we also have forgiven our debtors.
¹³ *And lead us not into temptation,*
        but deliver us from the evil one.'

¹⁴ *For if you forgive other people when they sin against you, your heavenly Father will also forgive you. ¹⁵ But if you do not forgive others their sins, your Father will not forgive your sins.*

¹⁶ *"When you fast, do not look somber as the hypocrites do, for they disfigure their faces to show others they are fasting. Truly I tell you, they have received their reward in full. ¹⁷ But when you fast, put oil on your head and wash your face, ¹⁸ so that it will not be obvious to others that you are fasting, but only to your Father, who is unseen; and your Father, who sees what is done in secret, will reward you.*

Study Questions

1. This passage from the Sermon on the Mount is not directed specifically to leaders, yet it provides good leadership principles. How would you summarize the message Jesus communicated?

_____

_____

_____

_____

_____

2. Why do you believe Jesus admonished people not to announce their giving? What happens in people when they give without letting others know about it? What changes in them?

_____

_____

_____

_____

_____

3. What can you learn from Jesus's admonition to pray and fast without letting others know about it? How can that be applied to leadership?

_____

_____

_____

_____

_____

❸ Paul Explains His Motives

1 Thessalonians 2:1–12

¹ You know, brothers and sisters, that our visit to you was not without results.
² We had previously suffered and been treated outrageously in Philippi, as you

know, but with the help of our God we dared to tell you his gospel in the face of strong opposition. ³ For the appeal we make does not spring from error or impure motives, nor are we trying to trick you. ⁴ On the contrary, we speak as those approved by God to be entrusted with the gospel. We are not trying to please people but God, who tests our hearts. ⁵ You know we never used flattery, nor did we put on a mask to cover up greed—God is our witness. ⁶ We were not looking for praise from people, not from you or anyone else, even though as apostles of Christ we could have asserted our authority. ⁷ Instead, we were like young children among you.

Just as a nursing mother cares for her children, ⁸ so we cared for you. Because we loved you so much, we were delighted to share with you not only the gospel of God but our lives as well. ⁹ Surely you remember, brothers and sisters, our toil and hardship; we worked night and day in order not to be a burden to anyone while we preached the gospel of God to you. ¹⁰ You are witnesses, and so is God, of how holy, righteous and blameless we were among you who believed. ¹¹ For you know that we dealt with each of you as a father deals with his own children,¹² encouraging, comforting and urging you to live lives worthy of God, who calls you into his kingdom and glory.

Study Questions

1. When Paul writes about his motives for working with the people of Thessalonica, what does he say he *has not* done? Why do you think he writes about this?

   _____

   _____

   _____

   _____

2. Paul describes his role with the people he led as being like a child and at the same time also like a parent. How can that be? What characteristics would you say apply to each?

   _____

   _____

   _____

   _____

3. Paul says that he and the other leaders "worked night and day in order not to be a burden to anyone." Do you think Paul's attitude in this respect is typical of most leaders? Explain your answer.

_____

_____

_____

_____

_____

4. What leadership lesson can you learn from Paul's example?

_____

_____

_____

_____

_____

LEADERSHIP INSIGHT AND REFLECTION

Do you think wanting to lead others is an advantage or disadvantage for someone in a leadership role? Explain.

_____

_____

_____

_____

_____

_____

How are people's motives to lead connected to their desire or lack of desire to lead?

_____

_____

_____

_____

_____

_____

What is your level of desire for leading people? Rate it on a scale of 1 (I never want to lead) to 10 (I greatly desire to lead in most situations). What are your motives? Describe them.

_____

_____

_____

_____

_____

How well do your motives align with the ones described by Jesus and Paul in the passages? In what ways do you need to change your thinking, mindset, or attitude to be in greater alignment with them?

_____

_____

_____

_____

_____

_____

TAKING ACTION

What is the most urgent or foundational change you need to make in your leadership motives? Be as specific as you can in describing it.

_____

_____

_____

_____

What immediate tangible step can you take to begin effecting that change? When will you take that step?

_____

_____

_____

_____

Group Discussion Questions

1. Do you think Jonah did not want to lead? Or do you think he simply did not want to do what God specifically asked him to do?

2. Do you naturally desire to lead or do you try to avoid leading when possible? Explain your answer.

3. How would you speculate that things ended up for Jonah? Do you think he learned from his experience and his heart softened toward God and the Ninevites? Or do you think he ended up bitter and resentful?

4. How difficult do you find it serve, help, or lead others without recognition? How do you keep yourself going and doing the right thing under those circumstances?

5. Paul said he worked night and day so that he would not be a burden on others. What actions could you take in your leadership to remove burdens from people?

6. What was your greatest takeaway about the right motives for leading others based on this lesson?

7. How do you believe God is asking you to change when it comes to your motives? What action will you take, and when will you take it?

LESSON 10

PRIDE

You Can't Fulfill Your Purpose
If You're Too Full of Yourself

THE ISSUE DEFINED

I once read that at the height of the Roman Empire, certain generals were honored with a *triumph*, a procession of honor through the city of Rome in which the general was preceded by marching legions, trumpeting heralds, and the enemies who had been conquered and captured in their victories. As the general rode in a chariot and was cheered by virtually everyone in the city, a slave held a laurel wreath above the general's head to signify his victory. But as the procession continued, the slave had one additional responsibility. He was to whisper the following words into the general's ear: "*Hominem te memento*," meaning, "Remember you are only a man."

Leaders can start to think that everything is all about them—especially when their team or organization is winning. The greater the accomplishment, the greater the temptation to take all the credit. That's why it's so important that they remain grounded. The most important quality of a well-grounded person is humility.

What is humility? Pastor and writer Rick Warren says, "Humility is not denying your strengths. Humility is being honest about your weaknesses. All of us are a bundle of both great strengths and great weaknesses, and humility is being able to be honest about both." Humility comes from that change in perspective, with the choice every day to give credit to God for our blessings and to other people for our successes.

Successful leaders are often put on a pedestal; to grow in humility, they need to intentionally climb down from it and get on the same level as those they lead. Humble leaders are comfortable with who they are and feel no need to draw attention to themselves. They revel in the accomplishments of others, empower others to excel, and allow others to shine.

The goal of leadership is to lift up people, not have them lift you up. When leaders allow others to put them on a pedestal, or if they minimize their own faults and overemphasize their successes, they create a Success Gap. That's a perceived distance between successful people and those who are less successful. When leaders *enjoy* that gap, they tend to protect their image, try to stay above the crowd, and work to make the gap look even larger.

In contrast, wise leaders are open about their failures and shortcomings. They use self-deprecating humor and laugh at themselves. They do everything they can to be themselves without pretense. Because they are not full of themselves, they are empowered to fulfill their purpose—and to help their people fulfill theirs.

CASE STUDIES

Read these case studies from the Bible and answer the study questions that follow.

① David's Humility and Gratitude, Even When God Denies His Request

1 Chronicles 17:1–27

¹ After David was settled in his palace, he said to Nathan the prophet, "Here I am, living in a house of cedar, while the ark of the covenant of the Lord is under a tent."

² Nathan replied to David, "Whatever you have in mind, do it, for God is with you."

3 But that night the word of God came to Nathan, saying:

4 "Go and tell my servant David, 'This is what the LORD says: You are not the one to build me a house to dwell in. 5 I have not dwelt in a house from the day I brought Israel up out of Egypt to this day. I have moved from one tent site to another, from one dwelling place to another. 6 Wherever I have moved with all the Israelites, did I ever say to any of their leaders whom I commanded to shepherd my people, "Why have you not built me a house of cedar?"'

7 "Now then, tell my servant David, 'This is what the LORD Almighty says: I took you from the pasture, from tending the flock, and appointed you ruler over my people Israel. 8 I have been with you wherever you have gone, and I have cut off all your enemies from before you. Now I will make your name like the names of the greatest men on earth. 9 And I will provide a place for my people Israel and will plant them so that they can have a home of their own and no longer be disturbed. Wicked people will not oppress them anymore, as they did at the beginning 10 and have done ever since the time I appointed leaders over my people Israel. I will also subdue all your enemies.

"'I declare to you that the LORD will build a house for you: 11 When your days are over and you go to be with your ancestors, I will raise up your offspring to succeed you, one of your own sons, and I will establish his kingdom. 12 He is the one who will build a house for me, and I will establish his throne forever. 13 I will be his father, and he will be my son. I will never take my love away from him, as I took it away from your predecessor. 14 I will set him over my house and my kingdom forever; his throne will be established forever.'"

15 Nathan reported to David all the words of this entire revelation.

16 Then King David went in and sat before the LORD, and he said:

"Who am I, LORD God, and what is my family, that you have brought me this far? 17 And as if this were not enough in your sight, my God, you have spoken about the future of the house of your servant. You, LORD God, have looked on me as though I were the most exalted of men.

18 "What more can David say to you for honoring your servant? For you know your servant, 19 LORD. For the sake of your servant and according to your will, you have done this great thing and made known all these great promises.

20 "There is no one like you, LORD, and there is no God but you, as we have heard with our own ears. 21 And who is like your people Israel—the one nation on earth whose God went out to redeem a people for himself, and to make a name for yourself, and to perform great and awesome wonders by driving out nations from before your people, whom you redeemed from Egypt? ²² You made your people Israel your very own forever, and you, LORD, have become their God.

²³ "And now, LORD, let the promise you have made concerning your servant and his house be established forever. Do as you promised, ²⁴ so that it will be established and that your name will be great forever. Then people will say, 'The LORD Almighty, the God over Israel, is Israel's God!' And the house of your servant David will be established before you.

²⁵ "You, my God, have revealed to your servant that you will build a house for him. So your servant has found courage to pray to you. ²⁶ You, LORD, are God! You have promised these good things to your servant. ²⁷ Now you have been pleased to bless the house of your servant, that it may continue forever in your sight; for you, LORD, have blessed it, and it will be blessed forever."

Study Questions

1. What prompted David to want to create a building to house the ark of the covenant? What was David's motive?

2. When David learned that God was not going to permit him to build a temple, what was David's response? What part of God's response did David focus on? Did David feel that he deserved God's kindness? What do these things say about David's character?

3. In verse 18, David says, "What more can David say to you for honoring your servant? For you know your servant." What did David mean by that? What has he implying?

_____

_____

_____

_____

_____

4. Why did David say in verse 25 that he had found courage to pray? Why did he need courage? What does that say about his perspective of God?

_____

_____

_____

_____

_____

_____

❷ Two Kinds of Leaders

Daniel 2:1–19, 24–49

¹ In the second year of his reign, Nebuchadnezzar had dreams; his mind was troubled and he could not sleep. ² So the king summoned the magicians, enchanters, sorcerers and astrologers to tell him what he had dreamed. When they came in and stood before the king, ³ he said to them, "I have had a dream that troubles me and I want to know what it means."

⁴ Then the astrologers answered the king, "May the king live forever! Tell your servants the dream, and we will interpret it."

⁵ The king replied to the astrologers, "This is what I have firmly decided: If you do not tell me what my dream was and interpret it, I will have you cut into pieces and your houses turned into piles of rubble. ⁶ But if you tell me the dream and explain it, you will receive from me gifts and rewards and great honor. So tell me the dream and interpret it for me."

7 Once more they replied, "Let the king tell his servants the dream, and we will interpret it."

8 Then the king answered, "I am certain that you are trying to gain time, because you realize that this is what I have firmly decided: 9 If you do not tell me the dream, there is only one penalty for you. You have conspired to tell me misleading and wicked things, hoping the situation will change. So then, tell me the dream, and I will know that you can interpret it for me."

10 The astrologers answered the king, "There is no one on earth who can do what the king asks! No king, however great and mighty, has ever asked such a thing of any magician or enchanter or astrologer. 11 What the king asks is too difficult. No one can reveal it to the king except the gods, and they do not live among humans."

12 This made the king so angry and furious that he ordered the execution of all the wise men of Babylon. 13 So the decree was issued to put the wise men to death, and men were sent to look for Daniel and his friends to put them to death.

14 When Arioch, the commander of the king's guard, had gone out to put to death the wise men of Babylon, Daniel spoke to him with wisdom and tact. 15 He asked the king's officer, "Why did the king issue such a harsh decree?" Arioch then explained the matter to Daniel. 16 At this, Daniel went in to the king and asked for time, so that he might interpret the dream for him.

17 Then Daniel returned to his house and explained the matter to his friends Hananiah, Mishael and Azariah. 18 He urged them to plead for mercy from the God of heaven concerning this mystery, so that he and his friends might not be executed with the rest of the wise men of Babylon. 19 During the night the mystery was revealed to Daniel in a vision. Then Daniel praised the God of heaven . . . .

24 Then Daniel went to Arioch, whom the king had appointed to execute the wise men of Babylon, and said to him, "Do not execute the wise men of Babylon. Take me to the king, and I will interpret his dream for him."

25 Arioch took Daniel to the king at once and said, "I have found a man among the exiles from Judah who can tell the king what his dream means."

26 The king asked Daniel (also called Belteshazzar), "Are you able to tell me what I saw in my dream and interpret it?"

²⁷ Daniel replied, "No wise man, enchanter, magician or diviner can explain to the king the mystery he has asked about, ²⁸ but there is a God in heaven who reveals mysteries. He has shown King Nebuchadnezzar what will happen in days to come. Your dream and the visions that passed through your mind as you were lying in bed are these:

²⁹ "As Your Majesty was lying there, your mind turned to things to come, and the revealer of mysteries showed you what is going to happen. ³⁰ As for me, this mystery has been revealed to me, not because I have greater wisdom than anyone else alive, but so that Your Majesty may know the interpretation and that you may understand what went through your mind.

³¹ "Your Majesty looked, and there before you stood a large statue—an enormous, dazzling statue, awesome in appearance. ³² The head of the statue was made of pure gold, its chest and arms of silver, its belly and thighs of bronze, ³³ its legs of iron, its feet partly of iron and partly of baked clay. ³⁴ While you were watching, a rock was cut out, but not by human hands. It struck the statue on its feet of iron and clay and smashed them. ³⁵ Then the iron, the clay, the bronze, the silver and the gold were all broken to pieces and became like chaff on a threshing floor in the summer. The wind swept them away without leaving a trace. But the rock that struck the statue became a huge mountain and filled the whole earth.

³⁶ "This was the dream, and now we will interpret it to the king. ³⁷ Your Majesty, you are the king of kings. The God of heaven has given you dominion and power and might and glory; ³⁸ in your hands he has placed all mankind and the beasts of the field and the birds in the sky. Wherever they live, he has made you ruler over them all. You are that head of gold.

³⁹ "After you, another kingdom will arise, inferior to yours. Next, a third kingdom, one of bronze, will rule over the whole earth. ⁴⁰ Finally, there will be a fourth kingdom, strong as iron—for iron breaks and smashes everything— and as iron breaks things to pieces, so it will crush and break all the others. ⁴¹ Just as you saw that the feet and toes were partly of baked clay and partly of iron, so this will be a divided kingdom; yet it will have some of the strength of iron in it, even as you saw iron mixed with clay. ⁴² As the toes were partly iron and partly clay, so this kingdom will be partly strong and partly brittle. ⁴³ And just as you saw the iron mixed with baked clay, so the people will be a mixture and will not remain united, any more than iron mixes with clay.

44 "In the time of those kings, the God of heaven will set up a kingdom that will never be destroyed, nor will it be left to another people. It will crush all those kingdoms and bring them to an end, but it will itself endure forever. 45 This is the meaning of the vision of the rock cut out of a mountain, but not by human hands—a rock that broke the iron, the bronze, the clay, the silver and the gold to pieces.

"The great God has shown the king what will take place in the future. The dream is true and its interpretation is trustworthy."

46 Then King Nebuchadnezzar fell prostrate before Daniel and paid him honor and ordered that an offering and incense be presented to him. 47 The king said to Daniel, "Surely your God is the God of gods and the Lord of kings and a revealer of mysteries, for you were able to reveal this mystery."

48 Then the king placed Daniel in a high position and lavished many gifts on him. He made him ruler over the entire province of Babylon and placed him in charge of all its wise men. 49 Moreover, at Daniel's request the king appointed Shadrach, Meshach and Abednego administrators over the province of Babylon, while Daniel himself remained at the royal court.

Study Questions

1. Why do you think Nebuchadnezzar asked the wise men to tell him his dream before interpreting it? What does his insistence on having them executed tell you about his character?

_____

_____

_____

_____

_____

2. How would you describe Daniel's attitude?

_____

_____

_____

_____

_____

3. What was Daniel's motivation for trying to interpret the dream? Why do you think he was willing to give it a try?

_____

_____

_____

_____

_____

_____

4. When Daniel successfully interpreted Nebuchadnezzar's dream, why do you think the king fell prostrate before him and paid him honor? How do you interpret it?

_____

_____

_____

_____

_____

_____

❸ Something to Be Proud Of

1 Corinthians 1:18–31

¹⁸ For the message of the cross is foolishness to those who are perishing, but to us who are being saved it is the power of God. ¹⁹ For it is written:

"I will destroy the wisdom of the wise;
*   the intelligence of the intelligent I will frustrate."*

²⁰ Where is the wise person? Where is the teacher of the law? Where is the philosopher of this age? Has not God made foolish the wisdom of the world? ²¹ For since in the wisdom of God the world through its wisdom did not know him, God was pleased through the foolishness of what was preached to save those who believe. ²² Jews demand signs and Greeks look for wisdom, ²³ but we preach Christ crucified: a stumbling block to Jews and foolishness to Gentiles, 24 but to those whom God has called, both Jews and Greeks, Christ the power of God and the wisdom of God. 25 For the foolishness of God is wiser than human wisdom, and the weakness of God is stronger than human strength.

26 Brothers and sisters, think of what you were when you were called. Not many of you were wise by human standards; not many were influential; not many were of noble birth. 27 But God chose the foolish things of the world to shame the wise; God chose the weak things of the world to shame the strong. 28 God chose the lowly things of this world and the despised things—and the things that are not—to nullify the things that are, 29 so that no one may boast before him. 30 It is because of him that you are in Christ Jesus, who has become for us wisdom from God—that is, our righteousness, holiness and redemption. 31 Therefore, as it is written: "Let the one who boasts boast in the Lord."

1 Corinthians 2:1–5

1 And so it was with me, brothers and sisters. When I came to you, I did not come with eloquence or human wisdom as I proclaimed to you the testimony about God. 2 For I resolved to know nothing while I was with you except Jesus Christ and him crucified. 3 I came to you in weakness with great fear and trembling. 4 My message and my preaching were not with wise and persuasive words, but with a demonstration of the Spirit's power, 5 so that your faith might not rest on human wisdom, but on God's power.

Study Questions

1. How does Paul describe the wisdom of the world and of human beings? Why does he describe them as he does?

_____

_____

_____

_____

_____

_____

_____

2. According to Paul, what's the one thing we should boast about? Why?

_____

_____

_____

_____

_____

_____

3. In Philippians 3:5–6, Paul gives his credentials: "circumcised on the eighth day, of the people of Israel, of the tribe of Benjamin, a Hebrew of Hebrews; in regard to the law, a Pharisee; as for zeal, persecuting the church; as for righteousness based on the law, faultless." However, in this passage he said he came to the Corinthians in "weakness with great fear and trembling." Why? Was he putting on a front? Or was he genuinely humble? Explain.

_____

_____

_____

_____

_____

_____

_____

_____

LEADERSHIP INSIGHT AND REFLECTION

David, Daniel, and Paul are three of the most accomplished and respected leaders in all the Bible, yet they exhibited great humility. Why?

_____

_____

_____

_____

_____

_____

_____

_____

Do you think they had to work at being humble, or do you think it came to them naturally? Explain your answer.

_____

_____

_____

_____

_____

_____

_____

_____

_____

_____

_____

In what aspects of your life are you humble? In what aspects do you take pride? Is that pride healthy? Is any kind of pride healthy? Explain.

_____

_____

_____

_____

_____

_____

_____

_____

_____

_____

How can leaders use humility in their leadership without being manipulative or false?

_____

_____

_____

_____

_____

_____

_____

_____

_____

TAKING ACTION

Would your family, friends, colleagues, and team members consider you to be proud, humble, or somewhere in between? Explain.

_____

_____

_____

_____

_____

_____

_____

How can you embrace genuine humility, keeping in mind the quote by Rick Warren: "Humility is not denying your strengths. Humility is being honest about your weaknesses. All of us are a bundle of both great strengths and great weaknesses, and humility is being able to be honest about both."

_____

_____

_____

_____

_____

_____

_____

_____

_____

What immediate step could you take with your team to demonstrate that humility genuinely?

_____

_____

_____

_____

_____

_____

_____

_____

GROUP DISCUSSION QUESTIONS

1. How do you think Nathan felt having to go back to David to say that God was not giving him permission to build the temple after having previously told the king, "Whatever you have in mind, do it, for God is with you"?

2. How much of Nathan's willingness to deliver the message was based on his courage, and how much was based on what he knew about David's character? What does this say about David's leadership?

3. How much of Daniel's willingness to deliver messages to Nebuchadnezzar was based on his courage, and how much was based on the king's character? What does this say about Nebuchadnezzar's leadership?

4. With whom do you most readily identify in the three passages: David, Nathan, Nebuchadnezzar, the wise men, Daniel, Paul, or the people of Corinth? Why?

5. In what part of your life do you most struggle with pride? What is the cause?

6. How would the development of greater humility benefit your leadership and improve your team?

7. What specific action do you believe God is asking you to take related to pride? When and how will you do it?

LESSON 11

CHOICES

The Decisions You Make, Make You

THE ISSUE DEFINED

The greatest power we have in life is the power to choose. Without question, our decisions are the biggest determining factor in how our lives turn out. Some people make their lives difficult by making wrong choices. Others move through life more easily because of the good choices they've made. All choices have consequences.

The reality is that we don't always get what we want, but we do always get what we choose. By choosing a course of action, a person chooses the results of that action. And recognize that not making a decision *is* a decision. In such situations, circumstances or other people end up choosing for us. It's much better to make decisions for ourselves.

The key to developing as a good decision-maker is to recognize that in every situation, we have some power to choose. Even in situations where we might feel powerless, we always have power over our own beliefs, feelings, and actions. Victimhood is a choice—and not a good one. Wise leaders never see themselves as victims of their circumstances. Instead, they work to discover their options in the midst of circumstances.

The choices that face leaders are not always easy. After all, when leaders are out in front, they are often breaking new ground, meaning there is no established path ahead. And that means making continual choices, many with very high stakes. A leader's choices impact not only them but also their followers. So it's always important to take into account how our decisions affect others. Wise leaders don't make followers pay the price for their bad choices.

Many leadership decisions carry a level of uncertainty and risk, but they still need to be informed decisions. It's important to research options, ask for and listen to advice, and predict possible outcomes. However, not every decision can be 100 percent certain before we have to make it. Leaders must balance planning ahead against paralysis of analysis. Often, the choice must be made with limited data. In those cases, it's wise to pray and draw conclusions based on what we do know, then choose the option with the greatest possibility of a positive outcome. And be sure to take action. Just saying you've decided, without doing anything about it, changes nothing.

If you want to know who the best leaders are, don't listen to what they say. Just examine the choices they make. And leaders' choices do more than *reveal* who they are; they also *determine* who they are—and will be. Every decision affects your future, your attitude, your character, and your level of influence. With each decision, we change—for better or worse.

CASE STUDIES

Read these case studies from the Bible and answer the study questions that follow.

① Moses Prepares to Say Farewell to the Israelites

Deuteronomy 30:1–20

¹ When all these blessings and curses I have set before you come on you and you take them to heart wherever the LORD your God disperses you among the nations, ² and when you and your children return to the LORD your God and obey him with all your heart and with all your soul according to everything I command you today, ³ then the LORD your God will restore your fortunes and have compassion on you and gather you again from all the nations where he scattered you. ⁴ Even if you have been banished to the most distant land *under the heavens, from there the L*ORD *your God will gather you and bring you back.* *5* *He will bring you to the land that belonged to your ancestors, and you will take possession of it. He will make you more prosperous and numerous than your ancestors.* *6* *The L*ORD *your God will circumcise your hearts and the hearts of your descendants, so that you may love him with all your heart and with all your soul, and live.* *7* *The L*ORD *your God will put all these curses on your enemies who hate and persecute you.* *8* *You will again obey the L*ORD *and follow all his commands I am giving you today.* *9* *Then the L*ORD *your God will make you most prosperous in all the work of your hands and in the fruit of your womb, the young of your livestock and the crops of your land. The L*ORD *will again delight in you and make you prosperous, just as he delighted in your ancestors,* *10* *if you obey the L*ORD *your God and keep his commands and decrees that are written in this Book of the Law and turn to the L*ORD *your God with all your heart and with all your soul.*

11 *Now what I am commanding you today is not too difficult for you or beyond your reach.* *12* *It is not up in heaven, so that you have to ask, "Who will ascend into heaven to get it and proclaim it to us so we may obey it?"* *13* *Nor is it beyond the sea, so that you have to ask, "Who will cross the sea to get it and proclaim it to us so we may obey it?"* *14* *No, the word is very near you; it is in your mouth and in your heart so you may obey it.*

15 *See, I set before you today life and prosperity, death and destruction.* *16* *For I command you today to love the L*ORD *your God, to walk in obedience to him, and to keep his commands, decrees and laws; then you will live and increase, and the L*ORD *your God will bless you in the land you are entering to possess.*

17 *But if your heart turns away and you are not obedient, and if you are drawn away to bow down to other gods and worship them,* *18* *I declare to you this day that you will certainly be destroyed. You will not live long in the land you are crossing the Jordan to enter and possess.*

19 *This day I call the heavens and the earth as witnesses against you that I have set before you life and death, blessings and curses. Now choose life, so that you and your children may live* *20* *and that you may love the L*ORD *your God, listen to his voice, and hold fast to him. For the L*ORD *is your life, and he will give you many years in the land he swore to give to your fathers, Abraham, Isaac and Jacob.*

Study Questions

1. As Moses neared death and knew that his time of leadership was coming to the end, he told the children of Israel they had a choice to make. They could turn toward God or away from him. What does Moses say will come to those who choose to love God, obey him, and keep his commands? What will come to those who don't? How do those promises translate to people today?

_____

_____

_____

_____

_____

_____

_____

_____

2. How does this important spiritual choice impact all the other choices people make as leaders?

_____

_____

_____

_____

_____

3. Moses warned that the Israelites would be tempted to bow down to other gods and worship them. What are the "gods" people bow down to today?

_____

_____

_____

_____

_____

_____

4. How do these other "gods" negatively impact people's leadership?

_____

_____

_____

_____

_____

_____

❷ A Warning that Helps with Decision Making

Proverbs 5:1–14

¹ My son, pay attention to my wisdom,
*   turn your ear to my words of insight,*
² that you may maintain discretion
*   and your lips may preserve knowledge.*
³ For the lips of the adulterous woman drip honey,
*   and her speech is smoother than oil;*
⁴ but in the end she is bitter as gall,
*   sharp as a double-edged sword.*
⁵ Her feet go down to death;
*   her steps lead straight to the grave.*
⁶ She gives no thought to the way of life;
*   her paths wander aimlessly, but she does not know it.*
⁷ Now then, my sons, listen to me;
*   do not turn aside from what I say.*
⁸ Keep to a path far from her,
*   do not go near the door of her house,*
⁹ lest you lose your honor to others
*   and your dignity to one who is cruel,*
¹⁰ lest strangers feast on your wealth
*   and your toil enrich the house of another.*
¹¹ At the end of your life you will groan,
*   when your flesh and body are spent.*

[12] *You will say, "How I hated discipline!*
How my heart spurned correction!
[13] *I would not obey my teachers*
or turn my ear to my instructors.
[14] *And I was soon in serious trouble*
in the assembly of God's people."

Study Questions

1. This passage admonishes us against the specific sin of adultery, but it also offers wisdom regarding more general decision making. What lesson can you learn about dealing with the offers that "drip honey" and are "smoother than oil" but lead only to bitterness and death?

2. The Proverbs writer, thought to be King Solomon, says, "Keep to a path far from her, do not go near the door of her house." What guideline or principle for dealing with temptation can you discern from this advice?

3. According to this passage, how will someone's life end if he makes bad choices? Based on verses 12 and 13, what could someone do proactively along the way to avoid that fate?

_____

_____

_____

_____

_____

_____

4. From this passage, what lesson can you learn regarding moral, personal, and leadership choices?

_____

_____

_____

_____

_____

_____

❸ A Governor's Tough Choice

Matthew 27:11–26

[11] *Meanwhile Jesus stood before the governor, and the governor asked him, "Are you the king of the Jews?"*

"You have said so," Jesus replied.

[12] *When he was accused by the chief priests and the elders, he gave no answer.* [13] *Then Pilate asked him, "Don't you hear the testimony they are bringing against you?"* [14] *But Jesus made no reply, not even to a single charge—to the great amazement of the governor.*

[15] *Now it was the governor's custom at the festival to release a prisoner chosen by the crowd.* [16] *At that time they had a well-known prisoner whose name was Jesus Barabbas.* [17] *So when the crowd had gathered, Pilate asked them, "Which one do you want me to release to you: Jesus Barabbas, or Jesus*

who is called the Messiah?" ¹⁸ For he knew it was out of self-interest that they had handed Jesus over to him.

¹⁹ While Pilate was sitting on the judge's seat, his wife sent him this message: "Don't have anything to do with that innocent man, for I have suffered a great deal today in a dream because of him."

²⁰ But the chief priests and the elders persuaded the crowd to ask for Barabbas and to have Jesus executed.

²¹ "Which of the two do you want me to release to you?" asked the governor.

"Barabbas," they answered.

²² "What shall I do, then, with Jesus who is called the Messiah?" Pilate asked.

They all answered, "Crucify him!"

²³ "Why? What crime has he committed?" asked Pilate.

But they shouted all the louder, "Crucify him!"

²⁴ When Pilate saw that he was getting nowhere, but that instead an uproar was starting, he took water and washed his hands in front of the crowd. "I am innocent of this man's blood," he said. "It is your responsibility!"

²⁵ All the people answered, "His blood is on us and on our children!"

²⁶ Then he released Barabbas to them. But he had Jesus flogged, and handed him over to be crucified.

Study Questions

1. What was Pilate trying to accomplish by asking the crowd to choose whether to release Jesus or Barabbas? What does this say about Pilate as a leader?

2. When Pilate's wife told him that Jesus was innocent, what do you think Pilate should have done?

_____
_____
_____
_____
_____
_____
_____

3. What was Pilate attempting to accomplish by washing his hands before the crowd? Did it work?

_____
_____
_____
_____
_____
_____
_____

4. In the Gospel of John, Pilate said, "What is truth?" (18:38). What does this statement tell you about Pilate's values? Based on the decisions he made in this passage from Matthew, what would you say was most important to Pilate as a leader?

_____
_____
_____
_____
_____
_____
_____
_____
_____
_____

LEADERSHIP INSIGHT AND REFLECTION

The three leaders in these passages—Moses, Solomon, and Pilate—had different approaches to how they made decisions. What would you say their criteria were? How were they different from one another? How were they similar?

When it comes to personal decisions, what criteria have you set for yourself?

What about as a leader? What criteria have you set for your leadership decisions?

Are these two sets of criteria the same, or are they different? Why? Are they in any way opposed to one another? If so, explain.

TAKING ACTION

Most people who experience a breakdown in their decision making do so either because they haven't determined their criteria, or they fail to follow through consistently using those criteria. Take some time to consider areas where you may be experiencing difficulties making choices. Then define the problem here. Do your difficulties come from lacking criteria or follow through?

_____
_____
_____
_____
_____
_____
_____
_____
_____

What do you need to change to become better at making decisions personally and professionally?

_____
_____
_____
_____
_____
_____
_____

What will you do about it, and when will you follow through?

_____
_____
_____
_____
_____
_____
_____

GROUP DISCUSSION QUESTIONS

1. With Moses stating that those who choose God will experience prosperity, be blessed, have large families, and have their fortunes restored, why do you think anyone would choose not to follow God?

2. The Proverbs passage focused primarily on moral choices. How do good and bad moral choices impact a person's leadership choices?

3. What is your opinion of Pilate? Was he a good leader who had to make a bad choice? A bad man who make an evil choice? An indifferent man who made a careless choice? An agent of God doing his will who really had no other choice? Or something else? Explain.

4. What do you think would have happened if Pilate had said Jesus was innocent and freed him?

5. When it comes to making choices, which best describes you:

   - prefer making a decision quickly, even if it's not the perfect decision.
   - make decisions based on the urgency of the situation.
   - prefer waiting as long as possible to make decisions while still meeting deadlines.
   - will take as long as needed to make the best possible decision.
   - prefer to let someone else make decisions.

6. What is your typical decision-making process? Before working on this lesson, had you previously developed your own criteria? If so, explain. If not, how do you plan to make choices in the future?

7. What change do you believe God is asking you to make to become a better decision maker? How and when will you make the change?

LESSON 12

CRITICISM

Action Always Causes Friction

THE ISSUE DEFINED

Greek philosopher Aristotle said, "Criticism is something you can avoid easily—by saying nothing, doing nothing, and being nothing." However, that isn't an option for anyone who wants to be successful as a leader. One of the prices of leadership is criticism. When spectators watch a race, where do they focus their attention? On the front runners! Few people pay close attention to the racers who are not in contention. Racers who are viewed as being out of the running are often ignored or dismissed. But when you're out front and ahead of the crowd, everything you do attracts attention. If you are successful, you *will* be criticized. People will always find something to be unhappy about.

Because criticism is a given in leadership, it's crucial to have a constructive strategy for dealing with it. Start by making sure you know and accept yourself. Self-knowledge and self-acceptance help in interpreting criticism accurately when it comes. Leaders who know themselves well are equipped to understand whether it's directed at them or at their role. They can also judge criticism against what they know to be true about themselves or the situation. If they're self-aware, they can determine whether the criticism is accurate and fair.

Wise leaders are always aware that the following things matter: the source, their attitude, and their intent. Correction from a trustworthy person, delivered with kindness and meant to be helpful, should always have more weight than a random potshot.

That being said, the truth of the message weighs even more than the delivery. Whenever criticism appears accurate and fair, no matter how, why, or by whom it was said, then it's the leader's responsibility to be open to it and learn from it. People can change for the better only when they are willing to improve. This is a matter of attitude. Wise leaders work hard to resist defensiveness, search for the grain of truth, figure out the changes they need to make, and take the high road in their response to the critic.

When criticism is unfounded and inaccurate, it is sometimes appropriate to respond with the truth, especially when the criticism is public, the source is influential, or the intent is constructive (since a person with that attitude would welcome correct information). But it's still wise to resist defensiveness and take the high road in the response.

When leaders allow and react appropriately to criticism, there is a very good chance that they will learn new things about themselves, improve in their leadership, and preserve their relationships. My friend Joyce Meyer observes, "God will help you be all you can be, but He will never let you be successful at becoming someone else." We can't do more than try to be all that we can be. We will sometimes take hits from others, but that's okay. That's the price for being out front.

CASE STUDIES

Read these case studies from the Bible and answer the study questions that follow.

① Learn to Accept God's Criticism First

Isaiah 30:8–22

> 8 "Go now, write it on a tablet for them,
>   inscribe it on a scroll,
> that for the days to come
>   it may be an everlasting witness.

⁹ For these are rebellious people, deceitful children,
   children unwilling to listen to the Lord's instruction.
¹⁰ They say to the seers,
   "See no more visions!"
and to the prophets,
   "Give us no more visions of what is right!
Tell us pleasant things,
   prophesy illusions.
¹¹ Leave this way,
   get off this path,
and stop confronting us
   with the Holy One of Israel!"

¹² Therefore this is what the Holy One of Israel says:

"Because you have rejected this message,
   relied on oppression
   and depended on deceit,
¹³ this sin will become for you
   like a high wall, cracked and bulging,
   that collapses suddenly, in an instant.
¹⁴ It will break in pieces like pottery,
   shattered so mercilessly
that among its pieces not a fragment will be found
   for taking coals from a hearth
   or scooping water out of a cistern."

¹⁵ This is what the Sovereign Lord, the Holy One of Israel, says:

"In repentance and rest is your salvation,
   in quietness and trust is your strength,
   but you would have none of it.
¹⁶ You said, 'No, we will flee on horses.'
   Therefore you will flee!
You said, 'We will ride off on swift horses.'
   Therefore your pursuers will be swift!
¹⁷ A thousand will flee
   at the threat of one;

at the threat of five
> *you will all flee away,*
till you are left
> *like a flagstaff on a mountaintop,*
> *like a banner on a hill."*

[18] *Yet the Lord longs to be gracious to you;*
> *therefore he will rise up to show you compassion.*
For the Lord is a God of justice.
> *Blessed are all who wait for him!*

[19] *People of Zion, who live in Jerusalem, you will weep no more. How gracious he will be when you cry for help! As soon as he hears, he will answer you.* [20] *Although the Lord gives you the bread of adversity and the water of affliction, your teachers will be hidden no more; with your own eyes you will see them.* [21] *Whether you turn to the right or to the left, your ears will hear a voice behind you, saying, "This is the way; walk in it."* [22] *Then you will desecrate your idols overlaid with silver and your images covered with gold; you will throw them away like a menstrual cloth and say to them, "Away with you!"*

Study Questions

1. Why is God criticizing the children of Israel in this passage? What have they done wrong?

_____

_____

_____

_____

_____

2. How do the people react and respond to God's criticism?

_____

_____

_____

_____

_____

3. How is God described by Isaiah in this passage? What does he say God wants to do for the people?

_____

_____

_____

_____

_____

4. What must the people do for God to be able to help them?

_____

_____

_____

_____

_____

❷ Jesus Warns His Followers to Expect Poor Treatment

Matthew 10:16–33, 38–42

16 *"I am sending you out like sheep among wolves. Therefore be as shrewd as snakes and as innocent as doves.* 17 *Be on your guard; you will be handed over to the local councils and be flogged in the synagogues.* 18 *On my account you will be brought before governors and kings as witnesses to them and to the Gentiles.* 19 *But when they arrest you, do not worry about what to say or how to say it. At that time you will be given what to say,* 20 *for it will not be you speaking, but the Spirit of your Father speaking through you.*

21 *"Brother will betray brother to death, and a father his child; children will rebel against their parents and have them put to death.* 22 *You will be hated by everyone because of me, but the one who stands firm to the end will be saved.* 23 *When you are persecuted in one place, flee to another. Truly I tell you, you will not finish going through the towns of Israel before the Son of Man comes.*

24 *"The student is not above the teacher, nor a servant above his master.* 25 *It is enough for students to be like their teachers, and servants like their*

masters. If the head of the house has been called Beelzebul, how much more the members of his household!

²⁶ "So do not be afraid of them, for there is nothing concealed that will not be disclosed, or hidden that will not be made known. ²⁷ What I tell you in the dark, speak in the daylight; what is whispered in your ear, proclaim from the roofs. ²⁸ Do not be afraid of those who kill the body but cannot kill the soul. Rather, be afraid of the One who can destroy both soul and body in hell. ²⁹ Are not two sparrows sold for a penny? Yet not one of them will fall to the ground outside your Father's care. ³⁰ And even the very hairs of your head are all numbered. ³¹ So don't be afraid; you are worth more than many sparrows.

³² "Whoever acknowledges me before others, I will also acknowledge before my Father in heaven. ³³ But whoever disowns me before others, I will disown before my Father in heaven. . . .

³⁸ Whoever does not take up their cross and follow me is not worthy of me. ³⁹ Whoever finds their life will lose it, and whoever loses their life for my sake will find it.

⁴⁰ "Anyone who welcomes you welcomes me, and anyone who welcomes me welcomes the one who sent me. ⁴¹ Whoever welcomes a prophet as a prophet will receive a prophet's reward, and whoever welcomes a righteous person as a righteous person will receive a righteous person's reward. ⁴² And if anyone gives even a cup of cold water to one of these little ones who is my disciple, truly I tell you, that person will certainly not lose their reward."

Study Questions

1. In this passage where Jesus is preparing the twelve disciples to be sent out to do his work, he tells them to be as shrewd as snakes and innocent as doves because he is sending them out like sheep among wolves. What do you think he meant? Why did he use *snakes* and *doves* in his description? How were they to be shrewd? How were they to be innocent?

2. If you're doing Christ's work and communicating his message, how does the passage say you should expect to be treated?

_____

_____

_____

_____

_____

3. What should your response be to the treatment you receive or that you anticipate receiving? How does Jesus say to handle it? And what makes that possible?

_____

_____

_____

_____

_____

4. Jesus said that students were not above their teacher, nor were servants above their master. How does this concept apply to leadership?

_____

_____

_____

_____

_____

_____

③ Peter Sets the Record Straight

Acts 11:1–26

¹ The apostles and the believers throughout Judea heard that the Gentiles also had received the word of God. ² So when Peter went up to Jerusalem, the circumcised believers criticized him ³ and said, "You went into the house of uncircumcised men and ate with them."

⁴ Starting from the beginning, Peter told them the whole story: ⁵ "I was in the city of Joppa praying, and in a trance I saw a vision. I saw something like a large sheet being let down from heaven by its four corners, and it came down to where I was. ⁶ I looked into it and saw four-footed animals of the earth, wild beasts, reptiles and birds. ⁷ Then I heard a voice telling me, 'Get up, Peter. Kill and eat.'

⁸ "I replied, 'Surely not, Lord! Nothing impure or unclean has ever entered my mouth.'

⁹ "The voice spoke from heaven a second time, 'Do not call anything impure that God has made clean.' ¹⁰ This happened three times, and then it was all pulled up to heaven again.

¹¹ "Right then three men who had been sent to me from Caesarea stopped at the house where I was staying. ¹² The Spirit told me to have no hesitation about going with them. These six brothers also went with me, and we entered the man's house. ¹³ He told us how he had seen an angel appear in his house and say, 'Send to Joppa for Simon who is called Peter. ¹⁴ He will bring you a message through which you and all your household will be saved.'

¹⁵ "As I began to speak, the Holy Spirit came on them as he had come on us at the beginning. ¹⁶ Then I remembered what the Lord had said: 'John baptized with water, but you will be baptized with the Holy Spirit.' ¹⁷ So if God gave them the same gift he gave us who believed in the Lord Jesus Christ, who was I to think that I could stand in God's way?"

¹⁸ When they heard this, they had no further objections and praised God, saying, "So then, even to Gentiles God has granted repentance that leads to life."

¹⁹ Now those who had been scattered by the persecution that broke out when Stephen was killed traveled as far as Phoenicia, Cyprus and Antioch, spreading the word only among Jews. ²⁰ Some of them, however, men from Cyprus and Cyrene, went to Antioch and began to speak to Greeks also, telling them the good news about the Lord Jesus. ²¹ The Lord's hand was with them, and a great number of people believed and turned to the Lord.

²² News of this reached the church in Jerusalem, and they sent Barnabas to Antioch. ²³ When he arrived and saw what the grace of God had done, he was glad and encouraged them all to remain true to the Lord with all their hearts. ²⁴ He was a good man, full of the Holy Spirit and faith, and a great number of people were brought to the Lord.

²⁵ Then Barnabas went to Tarsus to look for Saul, ²⁶ and when he found him, he brought him to Antioch. So for a whole year Barnabas and Saul met with the church and taught great numbers of people. The disciples were called Christians first at Antioch.

Study Questions

1. Why was Peter criticized? Was the criticism justified based on what his critics knew before he spoke to them?

_____

_____

_____

_____

_____

_____

2. How well do you think Peter handled the criticism? In what way did he address it? Why do you believe he spoke up?

_____

_____

_____

_____

_____

3. How did Peter's critics react to his explanation? What was the short-term result? What was the long-term result? What impact did Peter's initial actions in Joppa and later actions in Jerusalem have on the ministry of Saul? How did it ultimately affect the spread of the gospel?

_____

_____

_____

_____

_____

LEADERSHIP INSIGHT AND REFLECTION

Think about the three passages. In the Isaiah passage, the people were being criticized by God, their leader. In the Matthew passage, a group of potential leaders were being warned by their leader, Jesus, about forthcoming criticism because he himself had been criticized. And in Acts, the leader, Peter, was being criticized by a group within the church, an organization he was leading. What were the motives of the individuals doing the criticizing in the three passages? Were their motivations justified? Explain.

_____

_____

_____

_____

_____

_____

_____

In the Gospels, Jesus used parables to expose hypocritical leaders, but he also neglected to defend himself at his trial before his crucifixion. Given those facts, how should a leader handle unjustified criticism? How should a leader handle justified criticism? What criteria do you use to know how to respond to criticism?

_____

_____

_____

_____

_____

_____

_____

How do you typically respond to criticism?

_____

_____

_____

_____

_____

_____

TAKING ACTION

In what ways have your past reactions to criticism negatively impacted your leadership?

_____
_____
_____
_____
_____
_____
_____
_____
_____

What could you change in the way you respond to become a better leader?

_____
_____
_____
_____
_____
_____
_____
_____
_____

What change will you commit to, and when will you make it?

_____
_____
_____
_____
_____
_____
_____
_____
_____

GROUP DISCUSSION QUESTIONS

1. How do you reconcile Isaiah's assertion that God desires to be gracious and compassionate with his willingness to punish rebellion and disobedience? How can both be true?

2. Isaiah said the people relied on oppression and deceit and yet hoped to escape their consequences—"flee on horses." However, he said salvation was available instead through repentance and rest, and that strength would come from quietness and trust. Do you think those words apply to God's people today? If so, describe what repentance, rest, quietness, and trust look like.

3. Based on the Matthew passage, what is the role of the Holy Spirit when it comes to dealing with criticism?

4. In what ways have you relied on the Holy Spirit to help you deal with criticism? Can you give examples? How did they turn out?

5. Paul, called "Saul" in the Acts passage, later described himself as "the apostle to the Gentiles" (Romans 11:13). How do you think Peter's vision and his leadership decision to address his critics in Jerusalem impacted Paul's leadership?

6. What was your greatest takeaway about criticism in leadership from this lesson?

7. As a result of this lesson, what action do you believe God is asking you to take to grow as a leader? What will you do? When and how will you do it?

RECRUITING

No Team Can Succeed Without Good Players

THE ISSUE DEFINED

Professional sports organizations recognize the importance of selecting the right players. Every year, coaches and owners of professional teams prepare for the draft—the annual process of bringing in new prospects. First, they determine the positions that need filling. Then they send scouts to gather as much information as possible about potential recruits. Those scouts share information with team executives and coaches, who select the best players possible for their team. The future success of any team depends largely on their ability to draft effectively.

It's similar in business or ministry. Leaders must select the right players in order to create a winning team. Unfortunately, many leaders hire haphazardly. Because of desperation, urgency, or just plain ignorance, they quickly grab any candidate who comes along. Then they hold their breath and hope everything works out. But because they've rushed the process or chosen untested candidates, they often end up with players who can't help the team and may very well harm it.

It's critical for leaders in business or ministry to approach hiring in the same way winning coaches approach the draft: strategically. This begins with an accurate assessment of needs, with an eye toward the future and the big picture. What's the vision? How do you plan to achieve it? What tasks need to be done? What skills are deficient on the team? What weaknesses need to be shored up? Then candidates are identified (being sure to include team members already within the organization). This should be done by a leader who has demonstrated ability in spotting and evaluating talent. If good candidates are scarce or no one on your team is especially gifted at evaluating talent, you may want to enlist the help of a recruiter or a reputable hiring site or agency.

Of course, even the best recruits need to be developed. Wise leaders create and sustain a culture of development and growth, starting from the very top. As people are developed, they have the potential to rise through the organization. And recruiting from within is usually a shorter and easier process. Good recruitment is possible when done by the best leaders in the organization. When those leaders accurately determine needs, gather the right prospects, evaluate them effectively, and hire the best, the team is in a position to win big.

CASE STUDIES

Read these case studies from the Bible and answer the study questions that follow.

❶ Hiram Sends Huram-Abi to Solomon

2 Chronicles 2:1–18

[1] Solomon gave orders to build a temple for the Name of the LORD and a royal palace for himself. [2] He conscripted 70,000 men as carriers and 80,000 as stonecutters in the hills and 3,600 as foremen over them.

[3] Solomon sent this message to Hiram king of Tyre:

"Send me cedar logs as you did for my father David when you sent him cedar to build a palace to live in. [4] Now I am about to build a temple for the Name of the LORD my God and to dedicate it to him for burning fragrant incense before him, for setting out the consecrated bread regularly, and for making burnt offerings every morning and evening and on the Sabbaths, at the New Moons and at the appointed festivals of the LORD our God. This is a lasting ordinance for Israel.

[5] "The temple I am going to build will be great, because our God is greater than all other gods. [6] But who is able to build a temple for him, since the heavens, even the highest heavens, cannot contain him? Who then am I to build a temple for him, except as a place to burn sacrifices before him?

⁷ "Send me, therefore, a man skilled to work in gold and silver, bronze and iron, and in purple, crimson and blue yarn, and experienced in the art of engraving, to work in Judah and Jerusalem with my skilled workers, whom my father David provided.

⁸ "Send me also cedar, juniper and algum logs from Lebanon, for I know that your servants are skilled in cutting timber there. My servants will work with yours ⁹ to provide me with plenty of lumber, because the temple I build must be large and magnificent. ¹⁰ I will give your servants, the woodsmen who cut the timber, twenty thousand cors of ground wheat, twenty thousand cors of barley, twenty thousand baths of wine and twenty thousand baths of olive oil."

¹¹ Hiram king of Tyre replied by letter to Solomon:

"Because the LORD loves his people, he has made you their king."

¹² And Hiram added:

"Praise be to the LORD, the God of Israel, who made heaven and earth! He has given King David a wise son, endowed with intelligence and discernment, who will build a temple for the LORD and a palace for himself.

¹³ "I am sending you Huram-Abi, a man of great skill, ¹⁴ whose mother was from Dan and whose father was from Tyre. He is trained to work in gold and silver, bronze and iron, stone and wood, and with purple and blue and crimson yarn and fine linen. He is experienced in all kinds of engraving and can execute any design given to him. He will work with your skilled workers and with those of my lord, David your father.

¹⁵ "Now let my lord send his servants the wheat and barley and the olive oil and wine he promised, ¹⁶ and we will cut all the logs from Lebanon that you need and will float them as rafts by sea down to Joppa. You can then take them up to Jerusalem."

¹⁷ Solomon took a census of all the foreigners residing in Israel, after the census his father David had taken; and they were found to be 153,600. ¹⁸ He assigned 70,000 of them to be carriers and 80,000 to be stonecutters in the hills, with 3,600 foremen over them to keep the people working.

2 Chronicles 4:11–16

[11] So Huram finished the work he had undertaken for King Solomon in the temple of God:

[12] the two pillars;

the two bowl-shaped capitals on top of the pillars;

the two sets of network decorating the two bowl-shaped capitals on top of the pillars;

[13] the four hundred pomegranates for the two sets of network (two rows of pomegranates for each network, decorating the bowl-shaped capitals on top of the pillars);

[14] the stands with their basins;

[15] the Sea and the twelve bulls under it;

[16] the pots, shovels, meat forks and all related articles.

Study Questions

1. In the lesson on pride, you read that David wanted to build the temple, but God would not allow him to do it. As David's son Solomon prepared to start the project, he planned to gather resources and recruit workers. What does the number of people who were recruited and the way Solomon approached the process tell you about the young king's vision? What does it tell you about his leadership?

   _____

   _____

   _____

   _____

2. Why do you think Solomon approached Hiram king of Tyre to recruit skilled workers? What is the significance of Solomon detailing how he would compensate the workers?

   _____

   _____

   _____

   _____

3. Why do you think Solomon told Hiram that his own servants would work together with Hiram's?

_____

_____

_____

_____

4. The parallel account of the building of the temple in 1 Kings 7:14 says, "Huram[-Abi] was filled with wisdom, with understanding and with knowledge to do all kinds of bronze work. He came to King Solomon and did all the work assigned to him." What would have happened if this skilled craftsman had not assisted in the process?

_____

_____

_____

_____

_____

❷ Jesus Begins Choosing His Disciples

Luke 5:1–11

¹ One day as Jesus was standing by the Lake of Gennesaret, the people were crowding around him and listening to the word of God. ² He saw at the water's edge two boats, left there by the fishermen, who were washing their nets. ³ He got into one of the boats, the one belonging to Simon, and asked him to put out a little from shore. Then he sat down and taught the people from the boat.

⁴ When he had finished speaking, he said to Simon, "Put out into deep water, and let down the nets for a catch."

⁵ Simon answered, "Master, we've worked hard all night and haven't caught anything. But because you say so, I will let down the nets."

⁶ When they had done so, they caught such a large number of fish that their nets began to break. ⁷ So they signaled their partners in the other boat to come and help them, and they came and filled both boats so full that they began to sink.

8 When Simon Peter saw this, he fell at Jesus' knees and said, "Go away from me, Lord; I am a sinful man!" 9 For he and all his companions were astonished at the catch of fish they had taken, 10 and so were James and John, the sons of Zebedee, Simon's partners.

Then Jesus said to Simon, "Don't be afraid; from now on you will fish for people." 11 So they pulled their boats up on shore, left everything and followed him.

John 1:35–51

35 The next day John was there again with two of his disciples. 36 When he saw Jesus passing by, he said, "Look, the Lamb of God!"

37 When the two disciples heard him say this, they followed Jesus. 38 Turning around, Jesus saw them following and asked, "What do you want?"

They said, "Rabbi" (which means "Teacher"), "where are you staying?"

39 "Come," he replied, "and you will see."

So they went and saw where he was staying, and they spent that day with him. It was about four in the afternoon.

40 Andrew, Simon Peter's brother, was one of the two who heard what John had said and who had followed Jesus. 41 The first thing Andrew did was to find his brother Simon and tell him, "We have found the Messiah" (that is, the Christ). 42 And he brought him to Jesus.

Jesus looked at him and said, "You are Simon son of John. You will be called Cephas" (which, when translated, is Peter).

43 The next day Jesus decided to leave for Galilee. Finding Philip, he said to him, "Follow me."

44 Philip, like Andrew and Peter, was from the town of Bethsaida. 45 Philip found Nathanael and told him, "We have found the one Moses wrote about in the Law, and about whom the prophets also wrote—Jesus of Nazareth, the son of Joseph."

46 "Nazareth! Can anything good come from there?" Nathanael asked.

"Come and see," said Philip.

47 When Jesus saw Nathanael approaching, he said of him, "Here truly is an Israelite in whom there is no deceit."

48 "How do you know me?" Nathanael asked.

Jesus answered, "I saw you while you were still under the fig tree before Philip called you."

49 Then Nathanael declared, "Rabbi, you are the Son of God; you are the king of Israel."

50 Jesus said, "You believe because I told you I saw you under the fig tree. You will see greater things than that." 51 He then added, "Very truly I tell you, you will see 'heaven open, and the angels of God ascending and descending on' the Son of Man."

Study Questions

1. If you read only the account in Luke of Jesus calling his first disciples, you might think Jesus quickly chose Simon, but the account in John provides additional information. What steps were involved in the recruitment of Simon?

_____

_____

_____

_____

_____

2. Crowds of people were already following Jesus in both accounts before Jesus recruited anyone. Based on that information, what can you infer about Jesus, his recruiting process, and the people he chose?

_____

_____

_____

_____

_____

3. Simon was willing to put out into deep water and let down the nets only because Jesus said so. What does that tell you about Simon?

_____

_____

_____

_____

4. Jesus spent time with Andrew, and then Andrew went and found Simon. Jesus recruited Philip, and Philip recruited Nathanael. What lessons can you learn about recruiting from these events?

_____

_____

_____

_____

_____

3 A Team Is Recruited to Go to the Believers in Antioch

Acts 15:22–41

²² Then the apostles and elders, with the whole church, decided to choose some of their own men and send them to Antioch with Paul and Barnabas. They chose Judas (called Barsabbas) and Silas, men who were leaders among the believers. ²³ With them they sent the following letter:

> *The apostles and elders, your brothers,*
> > *To the Gentile believers in Antioch, Syria and Cilicia: Greetings.*
> > *²⁴ We have heard that some went out from us without our authorization and disturbed you, troubling your minds by what they said. ²⁵ So we all agreed to choose some men and send them to you with our dear friends Barnabas and Paul— ²⁶ men who have risked their lives for the name of our Lord Jesus Christ. ²⁷ Therefore we are sending Judas and Silas to confirm by word of mouth what we are writing. ²⁸ It seemed good to the Holy Spirit and to us not to burden you with anything beyond the following requirements: ²⁹ You are to abstain from food sacrificed to idols, from blood, from the meat of strangled animals and from sexual immorality. You will do well to avoid these things.*
> > *Farewell.*

³⁰ So the men were sent off and went down to Antioch, where they gathered the church together and delivered the letter. ³¹ The people read it and were glad for its encouraging message. *³²* *Judas and Silas, who themselves were prophets, said much to encourage and strengthen the believers.* *³³* *After spending some time there, they were sent off by the believers with the blessing of peace to return to those who had sent them.* *³⁴* *But Silas decided to remain there.* *³⁵* *But Paul and Barnabas remained in Antioch, where they and many others taught and preached the word of the Lord.*

³⁶ *Some time later Paul said to Barnabas, "Let us go back and visit the believers in all the towns where we preached the word of the Lord and see how they are doing."* *³⁷* *Barnabas wanted to take John, also called Mark, with them,* *³⁸* *but Paul did not think it wise to take him, because he had deserted them in Pamphylia and had not continued with them in the work.* *³⁹* *They had such a sharp disagreement that they parted company. Barnabas took Mark and sailed for Cyprus,* *⁴⁰* *but Paul chose Silas and left, commended by the believers to the grace of the Lord.* *⁴¹* *He went through Syria and Cilicia, strengthening the churches.*

Study Questions

1. Was the apostles' and elders' choice of Judas (called Barsabbas) and Silas random, or was there a reason they were chosen to go to Antioch? If so, what was their reason, and why was it important?

   _____

   _____

   _____

   _____

   _____

2. What value did Judas and Silas add to Barnabas and Paul? What value did they add to the believers in Antioch?

   _____

   _____

   _____

   _____

   _____

3. We get to see behind the scenes of recruitment in the early church through the interaction between Paul and Barnabas. What can you learn about recruiting from their disagreement? What can you learn about Paul and Barnabas?

_____

_____

_____

_____

_____

4. Would your perspective change if you knew that Paul's opinion of John (who was also called Mark) changed? Paul mentions twice that Mark is with him (Colossians 4:10; Philemon 24), and Paul asks for him in 2 Timothy 4:11, saying, "Get Mark and bring him with you, because he is helpful to me in my ministry." What can you learn from this change?

_____

_____

_____

_____

_____

LEADERSHIP INSIGHT AND REFLECTION

These passages show Solomon, Jesus, the apostles, Barnabas, and Paul recruiting people to help them. What criteria do you think each used? Note where different criteria were used to recruit various kinds of people.

_____

_____

_____

_____

_____

_____

_____

_____

_____

What can you learn from them? What was effective and what wasn't?

_____

_____

_____

_____

_____

When you have recruited people, what criteria have you used? Do you identify different criteria for different kinds of recruits? Explain. What has been effective and what hasn't? How would you rate yourself as a recruiter on a scale of 1 to 10, with 10 being the highest? Why?

_____

_____

_____

_____

_____

_____

TAKING ACTION

How could you improve as a recruiter? What would you have to do differently? What would you need to *start* doing and what would you need to *stop* doing?

_____

_____

_____

_____

_____

_____

What will you commit to do? When and how will you do it?

_____

_____

_____

_____

Group Discussion Questions

1. After Solomon gave the orders to start building the temple, what was the first thing he did? Why did he do it? What can you learn from this about leadership that is applicable today?

2. When the tabernacle was built under Moses's direction, the fine craftsmen and the workers were Israelites. But many of the people doing the work on the temple were foreigners. Why do you that was?

3. Nathanael was at first skeptical about Jesus, and Andrew spent a day observing Jesus, even after hearing John the Baptist call Jesus the lamb of God. Other disciples followed Jesus quickly and willingly. Some are named in the Bible, but the story of their recruitment is not told. How difficult do you think it was for Jesus to recruit the twelve? Explain your answer.

4. What is the role of recruiting in the communication and fulfillment of the gospel?

5. Who is the most talented recruiter you have worked with or worked for? What made him or her so good? What can you learn from that person? What skills or methods can you adopt?

6. What was your greatest takeaway about recruiting from this lesson?

7. In what way do you believe God would like you to improve as a recruiter? How would it improve your leadership? What will you do, and when will you do it?

LESSON 14

EQUIPPING

People Get Better When Their Leaders Want Them to Be

THE ISSUE DEFINED

Equipping is similar to training. But while training is focused just on learning specific job tasks, equipping is broader and deeper. You can compare it to what needs to happen to prepare people to scale a difficult mountain peak. It requires a process. Certainly, climbers need to be outfitted with equipment, and they also need to be trained in how to use it. But having the right tools doesn't guarantee they will make it up the mountain. Potential mountain climbers need to get into peak physical condition. They need to practice working within a team. They must be prepared to *think* like a mountain climber, so that they can trust and act on their instincts. All of these things require equipping.

When equipping potential leaders, the long-term goal is for them to become leaders in their own rights—to possess all the skills, attitudes, and instincts of a leader. It is much more than checking off a list of job skills or resources. There's no set formula. Instead, wise leaders focus on getting to know those they want to equip, then tailor their guidance to the individual's talents, strengths, and needs.

This process begins with an evaluation that takes into account the whole person: their natural gifts, personality, history, experience, and motivation. Then, with the overall goal of leadership development, and a thorough knowledge of the areas where the person needs to grow, the equipper creates a plan for growth. Together they set long-term and short-term goals.

The equipper provides tools and resources, along with opportunities to practice skills and make mistakes. Just like those who train people to become expert mountain climbers, wise leaders start by equipping their trainees in safe environments. The potential leaders learn and practice more skills along the way, growing in expertise with each "climb."

Throughout the process, the equipper provides consistent ongoing follow-up and accountability to help the emerging leader develop. The equipper also offers increasing amounts of responsibility and authority. Over time, the expectations and risks increase, and the challenges become more intense. Eventually, the equipping process produces an expert leader who can conquer even Mount Everest-sized challenges on his or her own.

CASE STUDIES

Read these case studies from the Bible and answer the study questions that follow.

① Moses Equips the Israelites to Equip Their Children

Deuteronomy 11:1–28

¹ Love the Lord your God and keep his requirements, his decrees, his laws and his commands always. ² Remember today that your children were not the ones who saw and experienced the discipline of the Lord your God: his majesty, his mighty hand, his outstretched arm; ³ the signs he performed and the things he did in the heart of Egypt, both to Pharaoh king of Egypt and to his whole country; ⁴ what he did to the Egyptian army, to its horses and chariots, how he overwhelmed them with the waters of the Red Sea as they were pursuing you, and how the Lord brought lasting ruin on them. ⁵ It was not your children who saw what he did for you in the wilderness until you arrived at this place, ⁶ and what he did to Dathan and Abiram, sons of Eliab the Reubenite, when the earth opened its mouth right in the middle of all Israel and swallowed them up with their households, their tents and every living thing that belonged to them. ⁷ But it was your own eyes that saw all these great things the Lord has done.

8 Observe therefore all the commands I am giving you today, so that you may have the strength to go in and take over the land that you are crossing the Jordan to possess, 9 and so that you may live long in the land the LORD swore to your ancestors to give to them and their descendants, a land flowing with milk and honey. 10 The land you are entering to take over is not like the land of Egypt, from which you have come, where you planted your seed and irrigated it by foot as in a vegetable garden. 11 But the land you are crossing the Jordan to take possession of is a land of mountains and valleys that drinks rain from heaven. 12 It is a land the LORD your God cares for; the eyes of the LORD your God are continually on it from the beginning of the year to its end.

13 So if you faithfully obey the commands I am giving you today—to love the LORD your God and to serve him with all your heart and with all your soul— 14 then I will send rain on your land in its season, both autumn and spring rains, so that you may gather in your grain, new wine and olive oil. 15 I will provide grass in the fields for your cattle, and you will eat and be satisfied.

16 Be careful, or you will be enticed to turn away and worship other gods and bow down to them. 17 Then the LORD's anger will burn against you, and he will shut up the heavens so that it will not rain and the ground will yield no produce, and you will soon perish from the good land the LORD is giving you. 18 Fix these words of mine in your hearts and minds; tie them as symbols on your hands and bind them on your foreheads. 19 Teach them to your children, talking about them when you sit at home and when you walk along the road, when you lie down and when you get up. 20 Write them on the doorframes of your houses and on your gates, 21 so that your days and the days of your children may be many in the land the LORD swore to give your ancestors, as many as the days that the heavens are above the earth.

22 If you carefully observe all these commands I am giving you to follow— to love the LORD your God, to walk in obedience to him and to hold fast to him— 23 then the LORD will drive out all these nations before you, and you will dispossess nations larger and stronger than you. 24 Every place where you set your foot will be yours: Your territory will extend from the desert to Lebanon, and from the Euphrates River to the Mediterranean Sea. 25 No one will be able to stand against you. The LORD your God, as he promised you, will put the terror and fear of you on the whole land, wherever you go.

[26] *See, I am setting before you today a blessing and a curse —* *[27]* *the blessing if you obey the commands of the Lord your God that I am giving you today;* *[28]* *the curse if you disobey the commands of the Lord your God and turn from the way that I command you today by following other gods, which you have not known.*

Study Questions

1. One of the challenges of equipping people is communication. How does Moses use history, vision, and connecting to help him communicate with the people in this passage? How does his communication equip the people for the future?

_____

_____

_____

_____

_____

_____

2. How does Moses prepare the people for experiences different from anything they have had before?

_____

_____

_____

_____

_____

3. Good leaders anticipate problems and prepare their people to meet them positively. What does Moses say in this passage to equip the people in this way?

_____

_____

_____

_____

_____

4. How does Moses equip the people to equip the next generation?

_____

_____

_____

_____

_____

❷ God Equips Joshua and Joshua Equips the People

Joshua 6:1–20

¹ Now the gates of Jericho were securely barred because of the Israelites. No one went out and no one came in.

*² Then the L*ORD* said to Joshua, "See, I have delivered Jericho into your hands, along with its king and its fighting men. ³ March around the city once with all the armed men. Do this for six days. ⁴ Have seven priests carry trumpets of rams' horns in front of the ark. On the seventh day, march around the city seven times, with the priests blowing the trumpets. ⁵ When you hear them sound a long blast on the trumpets, have the whole army give a loud shout; then the wall of the city will collapse and the army will go up, everyone straight in."*

*⁶ So Joshua son of Nun called the priests and said to them, "Take up the ark of the covenant of the L*ORD* and have seven priests carry trumpets in front of it." ⁷ And he ordered the army, "Advance! March around the city, with an armed guard going ahead of the ark of the L*ORD*."*

*⁸ When Joshua had spoken to the people, the seven priests carrying the seven trumpets before the L*ORD* went forward, blowing their trumpets, and the ark of the L*ORD*'s covenant followed them. ⁹ The armed guard marched ahead of the priests who blew the trumpets, and the rear guard followed the ark. All this time the trumpets were sounding. ¹⁰ But Joshua had commanded the army, "Do not give a war cry, do not raise your voices, do not say a word until the day I tell you to shout. Then shout!" ¹¹ So he had the ark of the L*ORD* carried around the city, circling it once. Then the army returned to camp and spent the night there.*

¹² Joshua got up early the next morning and the priests took up the ark of the LORD. ¹³ The seven priests carrying the seven trumpets went forward, marching before the ark of the LORD and blowing the trumpets. The armed men went ahead of them and the rear guard followed the ark of the LORD, while the trumpets kept sounding. ¹⁴ So on the second day they marched around the city once and returned to the camp. They did this for six days.

¹⁵ On the seventh day, they got up at daybreak and marched around the city seven times in the same manner, except that on that day they circled the city seven times. ¹⁶ The seventh time around, when the priests sounded the trumpet blast, Joshua commanded the army, "Shout! For the LORD has given you the city! ¹⁷ The city and all that is in it are to be devoted to the LORD. Only Rahab the prostitute and all who are with her in her house shall be spared, because she hid the spies we sent. ¹⁸ But keep away from the devoted things, so that you will not bring about your own destruction by taking any of them. Otherwise you will make the camp of Israel liable to destruction and bring trouble on it. ¹⁹ All the silver and gold and the articles of bronze and iron are sacred to the LORD and must go into his treasury."

²⁰ When the trumpets sounded, the army shouted, and at the sound of the trumpet, when the men gave a loud shout, the wall collapsed; so everyone charged straight in, and they took the city.

Study Questions

1. What do you think would have happened if God had not spoken to Joshua and given him specific instructions about how to conquer Jericho? How do you think Joshua would have approached the task? How do you think it would have turned out?

   _____

   _____

   _____

   _____

   _____

   _____

   _____

   _____

2. Why do you think God was so specific in his instructions to Joshua?

_____

_____

_____

_____

3. If you had been one of the people who received instructions from Joshua and marched around the city, what would you have been thinking?

_____

_____

_____

_____

_____

4. What do you think Joshua learned from this experience? What do you think the people learned? What knowledge, skills, or abilities do you think Joshua and the people gained from the Jericho experience that equipped them for success in the future ?

_____

_____

_____

_____

_____

_____

❸ The Greatest Sermon in History Contains Great Instruction

Matthew 7:1–29

1 "Do not judge, or you too will be judged. 2 For in the same way you judge others, you will be judged, and with the measure you use, it will be measured to you.
    3 "Why do you look at the speck of sawdust in your brother's eye and pay no attention to the plank in your own eye? 4 How can you say to your brother,

'Let me take the speck out of your eye,' when all the time there is a plank in your own eye? ⁵ *You hypocrite, first take the plank out of your own eye, and then you will see clearly to remove the speck from your brother's eye.*

⁶ *"Do not give dogs what is sacred; do not throw your pearls to pigs. If you do, they may trample them under their feet, and turn and tear you to pieces.*

⁷ *"Ask and it will be given to you; seek and you will find; knock and the door will be opened to you.* ⁸ *For everyone who asks receives; the one who seeks finds; and to the one who knocks, the door will be opened.*

⁹ *"Which of you, if your son asks for bread, will give him a stone?* ¹⁰ *Or if he asks for a fish, will give him a snake?* ¹¹ *If you, then, though you are evil, know how to give good gifts to your children, how much more will your Father in heaven give good gifts to those who ask him!* ¹² *So in everything, do to others what you would have them do to you, for this sums up the Law and the Prophets.*

¹³ *"Enter through the narrow gate. For wide is the gate and broad is the road that leads to destruction, and many enter through it.* ¹⁴ *But small is the gate and narrow the road that leads to life, and only a few find it.*

¹⁵ *"Watch out for false prophets. They come to you in sheep's clothing, but inwardly they are ferocious wolves.* ¹⁶ *By their fruit you will recognize them. Do people pick grapes from thorn bushes, or figs from thistles?* ¹⁷ *Likewise, every good tree bears good fruit, but a bad tree bears bad fruit.* ¹⁸ *A good tree cannot bear bad fruit, and a bad tree cannot bear good fruit.* ¹⁹ *Every tree that does not bear good fruit is cut down and thrown into the fire.* ²⁰ *Thus, by their fruit you will recognize them.*

²¹ *"Not everyone who says to me, 'Lord, Lord,' will enter the kingdom of heaven, but only the one who does the will of my Father who is in heaven.* ²² *Many will say to me on that day, 'Lord, Lord, did we not prophesy in your name and in your name drive out demons and in your name perform many miracles?'* ²³ *Then I will tell them plainly, 'I never knew you. Away from me, you evildoers!'*

²⁴ *"Therefore everyone who hears these words of mine and puts them into practice is like a wise man who built his house on the rock.* ²⁵ *The rain came down, the streams rose, and the winds blew and beat against that house; yet it did not fall, because it had its foundation on the rock.* ²⁶ *But everyone who hears these words of mine and does not put them into practice is like a foolish*

man who built his house on sand. 27 The rain came down, the streams rose, and the winds blew and beat against that house, and it fell with a great crash."

28 When Jesus had finished saying these things, the crowds were amazed at his teaching, 29 because he taught as one who had authority, and not as their teachers of the law.

Study Questions

1. This passage, which is from the Sermon on the Mount, contains a lot of instruction from Jesus. Why do you think Jesus covered so much ground?

_____

_____

_____

_____

_____

2. Review the passage and identify which parts contain general principles, which contain instruction for how to do tasks, and which contain warnings of things to avoid. Why did Jesus take these different approaches?

_____

_____

_____

_____

_____

3. How does someone benefit personally by living according to what Jesus taught? How would someone benefit as a leader? How would it help the team and the accomplishment of a team's mission?

_____

_____

_____

_____

_____

LEADERSHIP INSIGHT AND REFLECTION

How much of the equipping process comes from teaching principles, how much from specific instruction for doing tasks correctly, and how much from putting principles and instruction into practice? Explain your thinking.

_____

_____

_____

_____

_____

_____

Which type of equipping do you think is most difficult to teach: spiritual living, completing tasks, or leading others? Why? Which is more difficult to learn? Why?

_____

_____

_____

_____

_____

_____

_____

In what area of your life would you benefit from being better equipped? Who do you know who might be able to help you? Why should that person help you? What kind of time investment would you need? How would you benefit?

_____

_____

_____

_____

_____

_____

_____

Who has God put in your life who needs to be equipped? How could you equip them? How would they benefit? What are you willing to invest?

_____

_____

_____

_____

_____

_____

Taking Action

Plan to make two appointments this week. First, plan to meet with the person or people you are willing and able to equip. Tell them what potential you see in them and how you would like to help them. If they're willing, set up a regular time to invest in them. When will you meet with them, and how will you offer to help them?

_____

_____

_____

_____

_____

_____

_____

Next, request a meeting with people who might be willing to equip you. If they will meet with you, tell them what you admire about them in the area where you need to be equipped, how you hope to be helped, and how others will benefit from their investment in you. When will you request that appointment, and how will you ask them to help you?

_____

_____

_____

_____

_____

_____

_____

GROUP DISCUSSION QUESTIONS

1. In the passage from Deuteronomy, Moses was equipping the children of Israel so that they could equip the next generation who had grown up after the events of Egypt. What problems do leaders face when they are equipping people who lack common history with those equipping them?

2. As a leader, communicator, and equipper, how do you deal with those problems?

3. The Joshua passage includes Joshua's communication to the people and their follow-up actions, but his instructions to march around Jericho must have seemed peculiar. What kind of pushback do you think Joshua received? How do you think he handled it?

4. Of the teachings Jesus delivered in this section of the Sermon on the Mount, which do you find to be most insightful and helpful about how to live?

5. Which of the teachings do you find to be the most difficult to follow? Why?

6. Who in your past has done a good job of equipping you—for simple tasks, spiritual living, complex problems, or leadership responsibilities? What made that person a good equipper?

7. What can you learn from that experience? How can you use it to equip others? How will you do that?

LESSON 15

TEAMWORK

If People Don't Work Together, the Team Will Fall Apart

THE ISSUE DEFINED

Great challenges require great teamwork, and the quality most needed on a team facing a difficult challenge is collaboration. Notice that I didn't say "cooperation," because collaboration is more than that. Cooperation is working together agreeably. Collaboration is working together aggressively. Each person intentionally brings something to the table that adds value to the relationship and synergy to the team. As a result, the sum of truly collaborative teamwork is always greater than its parts.

Wise leaders emphasize collaboration when they encourage team members to focus on completing over competing. In any team, there is potential for competition. Siblings fight for their parents' attention. Coworkers compete for raises and promotions. Ballplayers go head-to-head for the chance to start instead of sitting on the bench. All individuals have hopes, goals, and dreams that they want to achieve. But on collaborative teams where team members work together, completing one another is more important than competing with one another.

For collaboration to work, teammates must be supportive rather than suspicious of one another. Some people are so preoccupied with looking out for their own interests that they are naturally suspicious of just about everyone, including their teammates. Supportiveness is a choice. It requires assuming that other people's motives are good unless proven otherwise. When leaders show support rather than suspicion, and insist on that same attitude from team members, it creates an atmosphere of trust and security.

Finally, effective leaders model a win-win mindset and expect it from everyone on the team. This is a belief that a win for the team can also be a win for every individual. With the goal of a team win in place, team members can change their attitude from one of "What's in it for me?" to "How does this benefit the team?" When people focus on the team and not just themselves, they share information, credit, and effort, with the goal of crossing the finish line together.

CASE STUDIES

Read these case studies from the Bible and answer the study questions that follow.

❶ Working Together Accomplishes Great Things

Nehemiah 2:17–20

17 Then I said to them, "You see the trouble we are in: Jerusalem lies in ruins, and its gates have been burned with fire. Come, let us rebuild the wall of Jerusalem, and we will no longer be in disgrace." 18 I also told them about the gracious hand of my God on me and what the king had said to me.

They replied, "Let us start rebuilding." So they began this good work.

19 But when Sanballat the Horonite, Tobiah the Ammonite official and Geshem the Arab heard about it, they mocked and ridiculed us. "What is this you are doing?" they asked. "Are you rebelling against the king?"

20 I answered them by saying, "The God of heaven will give us success. We his servants will start rebuilding, but as for you, you have no share in Jerusalem or any claim or historic right to it."

Nehemiah 3:1–32

1 Eliashib the high priest and his fellow priests went to work and rebuilt the Sheep Gate. They dedicated it and set its doors in place, building as far as the Tower of the Hundred, which they dedicated, and as far as the Tower of Hananel. 2 The men of Jericho built the adjoining section, and Zakkur son of Imri built next to them.

3 The Fish Gate was rebuilt by the sons of Hassenaah. They laid its beams and put its doors and bolts and bars in place. 4 Meremoth son of Uriah, the son of Hakkoz, repaired the next section. Next to him Meshullam son of Berekiah, the son of Meshezabel, made repairs, and next to him Zadok son of Baana also made repairs. 5 The next section was repaired by the men of Tekoa, but their nobles would not put their shoulders to the work under their supervisors.

6 The Jeshanah Gate was repaired by Joiada son of Paseah and Meshullam son of Besodeiah. They laid its beams and put its doors with their bolts and bars in place. 7 Next to them, repairs were made by men from Gibeon and Mizpah—Melatiah of Gibeon and Jadon of Meronoth— places under the authority of the governor of Trans-Euphrates. 8 Uzziel son of Harhaiah, one of the goldsmiths, repaired the next section; and Hananiah, one of the perfume-makers, made repairs next to that. They restored Jerusalem as far as the Broad Wall. 9 Rephaiah son of Hur, ruler of a half-district of Jerusalem, repaired the next section. 10 Adjoining this, Jedaiah son of Harumaph made repairs opposite his house, and Hattush son of Hashabneiah made repairs next to him. 11 Malkijah son of Harim and Hasshub son of Pahath-Moab repaired another section and the Tower of the Ovens. 12 Shallum son of Hallohesh, ruler of a half-district of Jerusalem, repaired the next section with the help of his daughters.

13 The Valley Gate was repaired by Hanun and the residents of Zanoah. They rebuilt it and put its doors with their bolts and bars in place. They also repaired a thousand cubits[c] of the wall as far as the Dung Gate.

14 The Dung Gate was repaired by Malkijah son of Rekab, ruler of the district of Beth Hakkerem. He rebuilt it and put its doors with their bolts and bars in place.

15 The Fountain Gate was repaired by Shallun son of Kol-Hozeh, ruler of the district of Mizpah. He rebuilt it, roofing it over and putting its doors and bolts and bars in place. He also repaired the wall of the Pool of Siloam, by the King's Garden, as far as the steps going down from the City of David. 16 Beyond him, Nehemiah son of Azbuk, ruler of a half-district of Beth Zur, made repairs up to a point opposite the tombs of David, as far as the artificial pool and the House of the Heroes.

17 Next to him, the repairs were made by the Levites under Rehum son of Bani. Beside him, Hashabiah, ruler of half the district of Keilah, carried out repairs for his district. 18 Next to him, the repairs were made by their fellow Levites under Binnuison of Henadad, ruler of the other half-district of Keilah. 19 Next to him, Ezer son of Jeshua, ruler of Mizpah, repaired another section, from a point facing the ascent to the armory as far as the angle of the wall. 20 Next to him, Baruch son of Zabbai zealously repaired another section, from the angle to the entrance of the house of Eliashib the high priest. 21 Next to him, Meremoth son of Uriah, the son of Hakkoz, repaired another section, from the entrance of Eliashib's house to the end of it.

22 The repairs next to him were made by the priests from the surrounding region. 23 Beyond them, Benjamin and Hasshub made repairs in front of their house; and next to them, Azariah son of Maaseiah, the son of Ananiah, made repairs beside his house. 24 Next to him, Binnui son of Henadad repaired another section, from Azariah's house to the angle and the corner, 25 and Palal son of Uzai worked opposite the angle and the tower projecting from the upper palace near the court of the guard. Next to him, Pedaiah son of Parosh 26 and the temple servants living on the hill of Ophel made repairs up to a point opposite the Water Gate toward the east and the projecting tower. 27 Next to them, the men of Tekoa repaired another section, from the great projecting tower to the wall of Ophel.

28 Above the Horse Gate, the priests made repairs, each in front of his own house. 29 Next to them, Zadok son of Immer made repairs opposite his house. Next to him, Shemaiah son of Shekaniah, the guard at the East Gate, made repairs. 30 Next to him, Hananiah son of Shelemiah, and Hanun, the sixth son of Zalaph, repaired another section. Next to them, Meshullam son of Berekiah made repairs opposite his living quarters. 31 Next to him, Malkijah, one of the goldsmiths, made repairs as far as the house of the temple servants and the merchants, opposite the Inspection Gate, and as far as the room above the corner; ³² and between the room above the corner and the Sheep Gate the goldsmiths and merchants made repairs.

Nehemiah 4:1–6

¹ When Sanballat heard that we were rebuilding the wall, he became angry and was greatly incensed. He ridiculed the Jews, ² and in the presence of his associates and the army of Samaria, he said, "What are those feeble Jews doing? Will they restore their wall? Will they offer sacrifices? Will they finish in a day? Can they bring the stones back to life from those heaps of rubble — burned as they are?"

³ Tobiah the Ammonite, who was at his side, said, "What they are building — even a fox climbing up on it would break down their wall of stones!"

⁴ Hear us, our God, for we are despised. Turn their insults back on their own heads. Give them over as plunder in a land of captivity. ⁵ Do not cover up their guilt or blot out their sins from your sight, for they have thrown insults in the face of the builders.

⁶ So we rebuilt the wall till all of it reached half its height, for the people worked with all their heart.

Study Questions

1. Look at the diversity of people who worked together to rebuild the wall. How many different regions are represented? How many different professions? How many of the tribes of Israel are mentioned? How many different classes of people? What does this say about Nehemiah's leadership that he was able to get so many different people to work together?

_____

_____

_____

_____

_____

_____

2. Why do you think they worked so well together? Why did they work with "all their heart" (verse 4:6)?

_____

_____

_____

_____

_____

_____

3. This passage ends with the wall being half completed. Nehemiah 6:15 states that they finished the task in remarkable time: "So the wall was completed on the twenty-fifth of Elul, in fifty-two days." Why do you think that was possible after the wall had lain in ruins for more than a century?

_____

_____

_____

_____

_____

_____

_____

② David and His General Rally the Troops

2 Samuel 10:1–19

¹ In the course of time, the king of the Ammonites died, and his son Hanun succeeded him as king. ² David thought, "I will show kindness to Hanun son of Nahash, just as his father showed kindness to me." So David sent a delegation to express his sympathy to Hanun concerning his father.

When David's men came to the land of the Ammonites, ³ the Ammonite commanders said to Hanun their lord, "Do you think David is honoring your father by sending envoys to you to express sympathy? Hasn't David sent them to you only to explore the city and spy it out and overthrow it?" ⁴ So Hanun seized David's envoys, shaved off half of each man's beard, cut off their garments at the buttocks, and sent them away.

⁵ When David was told about this, he sent messengers to meet the men, for they were greatly humiliated. The king said, "Stay at Jericho till your beards have grown, and then come back."

⁶ When the Ammonites realized that they had become obnoxious to David, they hired twenty thousand Aramean foot soldiers from Beth Rehob and Zobah, as well as the king of Maakah with a thousand men, and also twelve thousand men from Tob.

⁷ On hearing this, David sent Joab out with the entire army of fighting men. ⁸ The Ammonites came out and drew up in battle formation at the entrance of their city gate, while the Arameans of Zobah and Rehob and the men of Tob and Maakah were by themselves in the open country.

⁹ Joab saw that there were battle lines in front of him and behind him; so he selected some of the best troops in Israel and deployed them against the Arameans. ¹⁰ He put the rest of the men under the command of Abishai his brother and deployed them against the Ammonites. ¹¹ Joab said, "If the Arameans are too strong for me, then you are to come to my rescue; but if the Ammonites are too strong for you, then I will come to rescue you. ¹² Be strong, and let us fight bravely for our people and the cities of our God. The Lord will do what is good in his sight."

¹³ Then Joab and the troops with him advanced to fight the Arameans, and they fled before him. ¹⁴ When the Ammonites realized that the Arameans were fleeing, they fled before Abishai and went inside the city. So Joab returned from fighting the Ammonites and came to Jerusalem.

¹⁵ After the Arameans saw that they had been routed by Israel, they regrouped. ¹⁶ Hadadezer had Arameans brought from beyond the Euphrates River; they went to Helam, with Shobak the commander of Hadadezer's army leading them.

¹⁷ When David was told of this, he gathered all Israel, crossed the Jordan and went to Helam. The Arameans formed their battle lines to meet David and fought against him. ¹⁸ But they fled before Israel, and David killed seven hundred of their charioteers and forty thousand of their foot soldiers. He also struck down Shobak the commander of their army, and he died there. ¹⁹ When all the kings who were vassals of Hadadezer saw that they had been routed by Israel, they made peace with the Israelites and became subject to them.

So the Arameans were afraid to help the Ammonites anymore.

Study Questions

1. Which of David's actions in this passage are examples of good leadership to his team members?

_____

_____

_____

_____

_____

_____

_____

_____

2. What do you think of Joab's approach to leadership for the battle? Where did he rely on strategy? Where on relationships? Where on good execution by the team? Where on faith in God? What was the outcome?

_____

_____

_____

_____

_____

_____

_____

_____

3. Why did the teamwork of David's opponents break down? What went wrong? Could they have put themselves in a better situation? Explain.

_____

_____

_____

_____

_____

_____

_____

_____

③ Surviving Because They Worked Together

Acts 27:13–44

13 When a gentle south wind began to blow, they saw their opportunity; so they weighed anchor and sailed along the shore of Crete. 14 Before very long, a wind of hurricane force, called the Northeaster, swept down from the island. 15 The ship was caught by the storm and could not head into the wind; so we gave way to it and were driven along. 16 As we passed to the lee of a small island called Cauda, we were hardly able to make the lifeboat secure, 17 so the men hoisted it aboard. Then they passed ropes under the ship itself to hold it together. Because they were afraid they would run aground on the sandbars of Syrtis, they lowered the sea anchor and let the ship be driven along. 18 We took such a violent battering from the storm that the next day they began to throw the cargo overboard. 19 On the third day, they threw the ship's tackle overboard with their own hands. 20 When neither sun nor stars appeared for many days and the storm continued raging, we finally gave up all hope of being saved.

21 After they had gone a long time without food, Paul stood up before them and said: "Men, you should have taken my advice not to sail from Crete; then you would have spared yourselves this damage and loss. 22 But now I urge you to keep up your courage, because not one of you will be lost; only the ship will be destroyed. 23 Last night an angel of the God to whom I belong and whom I serve stood beside me 24 and said, 'Do not be afraid, Paul. You must stand trial before Caesar; and God has graciously given you the lives of all who sail with you.' 25 So keep up your courage, men, for I have faith in God that it will happen just as he told me. 26 Nevertheless, we must run aground on some island."

27 On the fourteenth night we were still being driven across the Adriatic Sea, when about midnight the sailors sensed they were approaching land. 28 They took soundings and found that the water was a hundred and twenty feet deep. A short time later they took soundings again and found it was ninety feet deep. 29 Fearing that we would be dashed against the rocks, they dropped four anchors from the stern and prayed for daylight. 30 In an attempt to escape from the ship, the sailors let the lifeboat down into the sea, pretending they were going to lower some anchors from the bow. ³¹ Then Paul said to the centurion and the soldiers, "Unless these men stay with the ship, you cannot be saved." ³² So the soldiers cut the ropes that held the lifeboat and let it drift away.

³³ Just before dawn Paul urged them all to eat. "For the last fourteen days," he said, "you have been in constant suspense and have gone without food—you haven't eaten anything. ³⁴ Now I urge you to take some food. You need it to survive. Not one of you will lose a single hair from his head." ³⁵ After he said this, he took some bread and gave thanks to God in front of them all. Then he broke it and began to eat. ³⁶ They were all encouraged and ate some food themselves.³⁷ Altogether there were 276 of us on board. ³⁸ When they had eaten as much as they wanted, they lightened the ship by throwing the grain into the sea.

³⁹ When daylight came, they did not recognize the land, but they saw a bay with a sandy beach, where they decided to run the ship aground if they could. ⁴⁰ Cutting loose the anchors, they left them in the sea and at the same time untied the ropes that held the rudders. Then they hoisted the foresail to the wind and made for the beach. ⁴¹ But the ship struck a sandbar and ran aground. The bow stuck fast and would not move, and the stern was broken to pieces by the pounding of the surf.

⁴² The soldiers planned to kill the prisoners to prevent any of them from swimming away and escaping. ⁴³ But the centurion wanted to spare Paul's life and kept them from carrying out their plan. He ordered those who could swim to jump overboard first and get to land. ⁴⁴ The rest were to get there on planks or on other pieces of the ship. In this way everyone reached land safely.

Study Questions

1. What evidence can you find in the passage indicating that the crew of the ship was accustomed to working together as a team?

_____

_____

_____

_____

_____

2. What instances can you find in the passage where teamwork was beginning to fall apart? Why was that happening? What was done to keep people working together?

_____

_____

_____

_____

_____

_____

_____

_____

3. What do you think would have happened if everyone had not continued to work together?

_____

_____

_____

_____

_____

_____

_____

4. How would you describe Paul's leadership in this incident? How did he get everyone to work together?

_____

_____

_____

_____

_____

_____

_____

_____

_____

LEADERSHIP INSIGHT AND REFLECTION

Based on your reading of these three passages, how do these factors come into play in leadership: God's direction, God's favor, vision, integrity and credibility of the leader, buy-in of team members, strategy, communication, relationships, collaboration, and execution? What other factors come into play?

_____

_____

_____

_____

_____

_____

_____

_____

When you are attempting to get people to work together as a team, how do you usually start the process?

_____

_____

_____

_____

_____

_____

_____

_____

Of the factors mentioned above, which do you rely upon? Where do you place the greatest emphasis for building the team and leading them to achieve success?

_____

_____

_____

_____

_____

_____

Which factors have you been neglecting?

_____

_____

_____

_____

_____

_____

TAKING ACTION

Based on your answers above, what should you be doing differently? How do you need to change your approach to team building?

_____

_____

_____

_____

_____

_____

_____

_____

_____

_____

What will you do differently? When and how will you do it?

_____

_____

_____

_____

_____

_____

_____

_____

_____

_____

GROUP DISCUSSION QUESTIONS

1. Was there a strategy in the way Nehemiah had the different groups build the different parts of the wall? If so, what was it? Why did it work?

2. Nehemiah and the people who returned to Jerusalem experienced opposition to their work. How commonly does that occur when a team is trying to get something done? What strategy did Nehemiah use for overcoming opposition?

3. How do you handle opposition when you're leading a team? What has worked well for you?

4. The main opposition Paul experienced in the third passage came from the forces of nature. How does that kind of difficulty need to be handled differently?

5. In the face of the storm, there were internal difficulties within the group Paul was trying to lead. How did Paul handle these difficulties?

6. What do you find most challenging when leading a team: external opposition, internal division, or forces beyond your control (such as nature)? Explain.

7. What is your greatest difficulty leading a team? How could you change to improve? What are you willing to commit to do? When and how will you do it?

LESSON 16

CONFRONTATION

When Things Go Wrong,
Leaders Work to Make Things Right

THE ISSUE DEFINED

Every person has problems and makes mistakes in the workplace. Every person needs to improve and needs someone to come alongside them to help them improve. As a leader, it is your responsibility and your privilege to be the person who helps your people get better. That often begins with a candid conversation.

So how does a leader handle being relational while still trying to move people forward? By balancing care and candor. Care without candor creates dysfunctional relationships. Candor without care creates distant relationships. But care balanced with candor creates developing relationships.

Caring values the person, while candor values the person's potential. It is important for you to value people. That is foundational to solid relationships. Caring for others demonstrates that you value them. However, if you want to help them get better, you have to be honest about where they need to improve. That shows you value the person's potential. And it requires candor.

One of the secrets of being candid is to think, speak, and act in terms of who the person has the potential to become and to think about how you can help them to reach it. Proverbs 27:6 says, "Faithful are the wounds of a friend, but deceitful are the kisses of an enemy" (NASB).

If you're candid with others but with their benefit in mind, it doesn't have to be harmful. It can be similar to the work of a surgeon. It may hurt, but it is meant to help and it shouldn't harm. As a leader, you must be willing and able to do that. If not, you won't be able to help your people grow and change.

Most leaders are facing a difficult conversation that they know they need to have but are avoiding. Usually they are reluctant for one of two reasons: either they don't like confrontation, or they fear that they will hurt the person they need to talk to. But if a leader can balance care and candor, it will actually deepen and strengthen the relationship.

The next time you find yourself in a place where you need to have a candid conversation, just remember this:

- Do it quickly—shovel the pile while it's small.
- Do it calmly, never in anger—balance care and candor.
- Do it privately—you want to help the person, not embarrass him or her.
- Do it thoughtfully, in a way that minimizes embarrassment or intimidation.

If your goal is to help the individual, improve the team, and fulfill the vision of the organization, then this is the path you should follow as a leader.

CASE STUDIES

Read these case studies from the Bible and answer the study questions that follow.

❶ Nehemiah Settles a Contentious Dispute

Nehemiah 5:1–19

¹ Now the men and their wives raised a great outcry against their fellow Jews.
² Some were saying, "We and our sons and daughters are numerous; in order for us to eat and stay alive, we must get grain."

³ Others were saying, "We are mortgaging our fields, our vineyards and our homes to get grain during the famine."

4 Still others were saying, "We have had to borrow money to pay the king's tax on our fields and vineyards. 5 Although we are of the same flesh and blood as our fellow Jews and though our children are as good as theirs, yet we have to subject our sons and daughters to slavery. Some of our daughters have already been enslaved, but we are powerless, because our fields and our vineyards belong to others."

6 When I heard their outcry and these charges, I was very angry. 7 I pondered them in my mind and then accused the nobles and officials. I told them, "You are charging your own people interest!" So I called together a large meeting to deal with them 8 and said: "As far as possible, we have bought back our fellow Jews who were sold to the Gentiles. Now you are selling your own people, only for them to be sold back to us!" They kept quiet, because they could find nothing to say.

9 So I continued, "What you are doing is not right. Shouldn't you walk in the fear of our God to avoid the reproach of our Gentile enemies? 10 I and my brothers and my men are also lending the people money and grain. But let us stop charging interest! 11 Give back to them immediately their fields, vineyards, olive groves and houses, and also the interest you are charging them—one percent of the money, grain, new wine and olive oil."

12 "We will give it back," they said. "And we will not demand anything more from them. We will do as you say."

Then I summoned the priests and made the nobles and officials take an oath to do what they had promised. 13 I also shook out the folds of my robe and said, "In this way may God shake out of their house and possessions anyone who does not keep this promise. So may such a person be shaken out and emptied!"

At this the whole assembly said, "Amen," and praised the LORD. And the people did as they had promised.

14 Moreover, from the twentieth year of King Artaxerxes, when I was appointed to be their governor in the land of Judah, until his thirty-second year—twelve years—neither I nor my brothers ate the food allotted to the governor. 15 But the earlier governors—those preceding me—placed a heavy burden on the people and took forty shekels of silver from them in addition to food and wine. Their assistants also lorded it over the people. But out of reverence for God I did not act like that. 16 Instead, I devoted myself to the work on this wall. All my men were assembled there for the work; we did not acquire any land.

17 Furthermore, a hundred and fifty Jews and officials ate at my table, as well as those who came to us from the surrounding nations. 18 Each day one ox, six choice sheep and some poultry were prepared for me, and every ten days an abundant supply of wine of all kinds. In spite of all this, I never demanded the food allotted to the governor, because the demands were heavy on these people.

19 Remember me with favor, my God, for all I have done for these people.

Study Questions

1. What reasons did Nehemiah have for confronting the nobles and officials? Were the reasons personal? Spiritual? Official?

   _____

   _____

   _____

   _____

   _____

2. What happened *before* Nehemiah confronted the nobles and officials? Describe the steps he went through.

   _____

   _____

   _____

   _____

   _____

3. How did the nobles and officials respond? Was the confrontation successful? How did Nehemiah's interaction further the vision? Explain.

   _____

   _____

   _____

   _____

   _____

4. How did Nehemiah's actions and personal modeling support his interaction with the officials and the people they led? What does this tell you about his leadership?

_____

_____

_____

_____

_____

② Jesus Teaches the Right Way to Confront

Matthew 18:15–35

[15] *"If your brother or sister sins, go and point out their fault, just between the two of you. If they listen to you, you have won them over.* [16] *But if they will not listen, take one or two others along, so that 'every matter may be established by the testimony of two or three witnesses.'* [17] *If they still refuse to listen, tell it to the church; and if they refuse to listen even to the church, treat them as you would a pagan or a tax collector.*

[18] *"Truly I tell you, whatever you bind on earth will be bound in heaven, and whatever you loose on earth will be loosed in heaven.*

[19] *"Again, truly I tell you that if two of you on earth agree about anything they ask for, it will be done for them by my Father in heaven.* [20] *For where two or three gather in my name, there am I with them."*

[21] *Then Peter came to Jesus and asked, "Lord, how many times shall I forgive my brother or sister who sins against me? Up to seven times?"*

[22] *Jesus answered, "I tell you, not seven times, but seventy-seven times.*

[23] *"Therefore, the kingdom of heaven is like a king who wanted to settle accounts with his servants.* [24] *As he began the settlement, a man who owed him ten thousand bags of gold was brought to him.* [25] *Since he was not able to pay, the master ordered that he and his wife and his children and all that he had be sold to repay the debt.*

[26] *"At this the servant fell on his knees before him. 'Be patient with me,' he begged, 'and I will pay back everything.'* [27] *The servant's master took pity on him, canceled the debt and let him go.*

28 "But when that servant went out, he found one of his fellow servants who owed him a hundred silver coins. He grabbed him and began to choke him. 'Pay back what you owe me!' he demanded.

29 "His fellow servant fell to his knees and begged him, 'Be patient with me, and I will pay it back.'

30 "But he refused. Instead, he went off and had the man thrown into prison until he could pay the debt. 31 When the other servants saw what had happened, they were outraged and went and told their master everything that had happened.

32 "Then the master called the servant in. 'You wicked servant,' he said, 'I canceled all that debt of yours because you begged me to. 33 Shouldn't you have had mercy on your fellow servant just as I had on you?' 34 In anger his master handed him over to the jailers to be tortured, until he should pay back all he owed.

35 "This is how my heavenly Father will treat each of you unless you forgive your brother or sister from your heart."

Study Questions

1. According to the passage, what steps are you to follow in confronting someone? Write them here.

_____

_____

_____

_____

_____

2. Some manuscripts of this passage use the phrase "sins against you." Are there other situations where this same process of confrontation would be appropriate and helpful? If so, explain.

_____

_____

_____

_____

_____

3. The emphasis in this passage is on mercy and forgiveness. Why? How should these ideas influence our goals for confronting?

_____

_____

_____

_____

_____

_____

4. Jesus tells Peter he should forgive someone who sins against him seventy-seven times. How difficult do you find it to follow that advice? What do you do personally to be able to better live out what Jesus says to do?

_____

_____

_____

_____

_____

③ Restoration Is the Best Outcome

Galatians 6:1–10

¹ Brothers and sisters, if someone is caught in a sin, you who live by the Spirit should restore that person gently. But watch yourselves, or you also may be tempted. ² Carry each other's burdens, and in this way you will fulfill the law of Christ. ³ If anyone thinks they are something when they are not, they deceive themselves. ⁴ Each one should test their own actions. Then they can take pride in themselves alone, without comparing themselves to someone else, ⁵ for each one should carry their own load. ⁶ Nevertheless, the one who receives instruction in the word should share all good things with their instructor.

⁷ Do not be deceived: God cannot be mocked. A man reaps what he sows. ⁸ Whoever sows to please their flesh, from the flesh will reap destruction; whoever sows to please the Spirit, from the Spirit will reap eternal life. ⁹ Let us not become weary in doing good, for at the proper time we will reap a harvest if we do not give up. ¹⁰ Therefore, as we have opportunity, let us do good to all people, especially to those who belong to the family of believers.

Study Questions

1. In this passage written by Paul to the Galatians, what do you think it means to carry each other's burdens? What is the appropriate way for leaders to do that?

   _____

   _____

   _____

   _____

   _____

2. The passage mentions the problems of self-deception, self-importance, and comparison of self to others. How do these issues come into play with people who get off track and need to be confronted? Why does Paul warn those who confront against temptation?

   _____

   _____

   _____

   _____

   _____

   _____

3. Paul states that our goal should be to gently restore people who do wrong. But he also says that people reap what they sow. How do you reconcile these ideas? What is your role in confrontation, what is the role of the person being confronted, and what is God's role?

   _____

   _____

   _____

   _____

   _____

LEADERSHIP INSIGHT AND REFLECTION

Based on your reading of the three passages, what responsibility do people of faith have to gently confront others when they do wrong?

_____

_____

_____

_____

_____

_____

_____

_____

_____

_____

Do leaders have more, less, or the same level of responsibility for confronting problems and wrongdoing? Explain.

_____

_____

_____

_____

_____

_____

_____

_____

_____

In your capacity as a leader, what kinds of things should you confront? Why? What kinds of things should you not confront? Why?

_____

_____

_____

_____

_____

_____

_____

_____

Write a personal code of conduct for confronting people you lead. Include what, when, and how you should confront people, as well as the outcome you will always strive to achieve.

_____

_____

_____

_____

_____

_____

_____

_____

_____

_____

TAKING ACTION

Based on your code of conduct and your answers related to the responsibility to confront, is there someone you should confront but haven't? If so, who is it, and why should you be confronting him or her?

_____

_____

_____

_____

_____

_____

_____

_____

_____

_____

_____

_____

_____

_____

When is the soonest you can meet privately with this person face to face?

_____

_____

_____

_____

When will you make the appointment?

_____

_____

_____

After the meeting, write your observations about what went well, what didn't, and how you can do a better job next time.

_____

_____

_____

_____

_____

_____

_____

_____

_____

_____

_____

_____

_____

_____

_____

_____

_____

_____

_____

_____

_____

GROUP DISCUSSION QUESTIONS

1. In the first passage, Nehemiah, as the appointed governor, was dealing with a complaint from people about their leaders. What are some of the challenges of fielding complaints between followers and their leaders?

2. In the second passage, Jesus tells people to be proactive in confronting others who do wrong. Is proactive confrontation different from reactive confrontation? If so, how?

3. When following the instructions that Jesus gives in Matthew 18:15–17, what would you say are the goals of confrontation?

4. In the context of confronting others and forgiving, why did Jesus tell the parable about the unmerciful servant who was forgiven but refused to forgive others? What are we to take away from that?

5. Which do you find more difficult: confronting others when there's a problem or being confronted when you've done something wrong? Explain your answer.

6. What was your greatest takeaway about confrontation from this lesson?

7. Where do you most need to grow when it comes to confrontation? What action can you take to improve? When and how will you do it?

LESSON 17

MENTORING

Investing in People Provides
the Greatest Leadership Return

THE ISSUE DEFINED

If equipping is like preparing people to become expert mountain climbers, then mentoring is like training them to become something more: the best version of themselves, both on the mountain and off. This involves helping them grow holistically—developing personal qualities that will benefit them in many areas of life, not just in their job requirements.

Because mentoring involves the whole person, it is even more difficult and time-consuming than equipping. It's also extremely personalized, because it's not about developing a skill set that leads to expertise in a specific area. It's about helping the person grow as a unique individual, in many areas of life. This requires an even deeper understanding of—and investment in—them, knowing their strengths, weaknesses, needs, and desires.

Like equipping, mentoring takes time. Unlike equipping, it doesn't always have a measurable outcome or a clear deadline. So it's especially important with mentoring to focus on the journey more than the destination. Fortunately, mentoring people does have some specific steps that can be taken: getting to know them, finding out their goals and desires for growth, spending time together, answering questions, challenging them. However, it's not one-size-fits-all. After all, different people don't necessarily respond to the same types of guidance. However, certain behaviors should be demonstrated with everyone: consistency, kindness, respect.

Mentoring is customized to the person being mentored. It's not realistic to expect to use the same strategies and methods with all people. One person will respond well to being challenged; another will need to be nurtured. One will need the game plan drawn up; another will be more passionate about creating that game plan. One will require consistent, frequent follow-up; another will require breathing room. It's important to tailor the mentoring style to what someone needs.

It often works to think of mentoring as a combination of teaching, demonstration, observation, and follow-up. Good mentors both consistently model and clearly explain right behaviors. They provide opportunities to practice what's been taught. And afterward, they talk together and draw conclusions about the outcomes. Growth can result from both positive and negative outcomes. So while much of growth comes through choosing a positive response to failing or losing, it's equally important to respond appropriately to winning.

When leaders dedicate themselves to mentoring and commit to it as a long-term process, a change occurs in their relationships with their people. Followers who are effectively mentored develop a deep loyalty, because they have proof the leader has their best interests at heart. Even when followers have to move on, they often desire to maintain an ongoing relationship with their mentor. New mentees, after witnessing the successful mentoring of others, are eager to step up. Leaders who mentor well are able to develop a culture of mentoring that extends throughout the organization. And when everyone is becoming the best they can be, the organization does the same.

CASE STUDIES

Read these case studies from the Bible and answer the study questions that follow.

① Leaders Who Disqualify Themselves from Mentoring Others

Luke 11:37–54

37 When Jesus had finished speaking, a Pharisee invited him to eat with him; so he went in and reclined at the table. 38 But the Pharisee was surprised when he noticed that Jesus did not first wash before the meal.

39 Then the Lord said to him, "Now then, you Pharisees clean the outside of the cup and dish, but inside you are full of greed and wickedness. 40 You foolish people! Did not the one who made the outside make the inside also? 41 But now as for what is inside you—be generous to the poor, and everything will be clean for you.

42 "Woe to you Pharisees, because you give God a tenth of your mint, rue and all other kinds of garden herbs, but you neglect justice and the love of God. You should have practiced the latter without leaving the former undone.

43 "Woe to you Pharisees, because you love the most important seats in the synagogues and respectful greetings in the marketplaces.

44 "Woe to you, because you are like unmarked graves, which people walk over without knowing it."

45 One of the experts in the law answered him, "Teacher, when you say these things, you insult us also."

46 Jesus replied, "And you experts in the law, woe to you, because you load people down with burdens they can hardly carry, and you yourselves will not lift one finger to help them.

47 "Woe to you, because you build tombs for the prophets, and it was your ancestors who killed them. 48 So you testify that you approve of what your ancestors did; they killed the prophets, and you build their tombs. 49 Because of this, God in his wisdom said, 'I will send them prophets and apostles, some of whom they will kill and others they will persecute.'

50 "Therefore this generation will be held responsible for the blood of all the prophets that has been shed since the beginning of the world, 51 from the blood of Abel to the blood of Zechariah, who was killed between the altar and the sanctuary. Yes, I tell you, this generation will be held responsible for it all.

52 "Woe to you experts in the law, because you have taken away the key to knowledge. You yourselves have not entered, and you have hindered those who were entering."

53 When Jesus went outside, the Pharisees and the teachers of the law began to oppose him fiercely and to besiege him with questions, 54 waiting to catch him in something he might say.

Study Questions

1. When the Pharisees criticized Jesus for not washing before a meal, he pointed out where their thinking and practices were wrong. What was their response? And how did the experts in the law respond?

_____

_____

_____

_____

_____

_____

2. The Pharisees and experts in the law had positions of authority, yet they were not worthy of being mentors. Why? List all the reasons in the passage that would disqualify them.

_____

_____

_____

_____

_____

_____

_____

3. God sent the prophets to instruct and direct the religious leaders. How does Jesus say they responded to the prophets? What does this tell you about the religious leaders of Jesus's day?

_____

_____

_____

_____

_____

_____

4. Jesus said to these authorities, "You have taken away the key to knowledge. You yourselves have not entered, and you have hindered those who were entering." Have you encountered or observed leaders who do this? If so, how do the people they lead respond?

_____

_____

_____

_____

_____

❷ A Pharisee Comes to Learn from Jesus

John 3:1–21

¹ Now there was a Pharisee, a man named Nicodemus who was a member of the Jewish ruling council. ² He came to Jesus at night and said, "Rabbi, we know that you are a teacher who has come from God. For no one could perform the signs you are doing if God were not with him."

³ Jesus replied, "Very truly I tell you, no one can see the kingdom of God unless they are born again."

⁴ "How can someone be born when they are old?" Nicodemus asked. "Surely they cannot enter a second time into their mother's womb to be born!"

⁵ Jesus answered, "Very truly I tell you, no one can enter the kingdom of God unless they are born of water and the Spirit. ⁶ Flesh gives birth to flesh, but the Spirit gives birth to spirit. ⁷ You should not be surprised at my saying, 'You must be born again.' ⁸ The wind blows wherever it pleases. You hear its sound, but you cannot tell where it comes from or where it is going. So it is with everyone born of the Spirit."

⁹ "How can this be?" Nicodemus asked.

¹⁰ "You are Israel's teacher," said Jesus, "and do you not understand these things? ¹¹ Very truly I tell you, we speak of what we know, and we testify to what we have seen, but still you people do not accept our testimony. ¹² I have spoken to you of earthly things and you do not believe; how then will you believe if I speak of heavenly things? ¹³ No one has ever gone into heaven except the one who came from heaven—the Son of Man. ¹⁴ Just as Moses lifted up the snake in the wilderness, so the Son of Man must be lifted up, ¹⁵ that everyone who believes may have eternal life in him."

¹⁶ For God so loved the world that he gave his one and only Son, that whoever believes in him shall not perish but have eternal life. ¹⁷ For God did not send his Son into the world to condemn the world, but to save the world through him. ¹⁸ Whoever believes in him is not condemned, but whoever does not believe stands condemned already because they have not believed in the name of God's one and only Son. ¹⁹ This is the verdict: Light has come into the world, but people loved darkness instead of light because their deeds were evil. ²⁰ Everyone who does evil hates the light, and will not come into the light for fear that their deeds will be exposed. ²¹ But whoever lives by the truth comes into the light, so that it may be seen plainly that what they have done has been done in the sight of God.

Study Questions

1. In this passage, Nicodemus sought out Jesus and immediately acknowledged Jesus's authority. Why did Jesus immediately challenge his thinking by telling him people must be born again to see the kingdom of God?

2. Often when he was asked questions, Jesus responded by asking a question or he told a parable. In this case, he answered Nicodemus directly with an explanation. Why? Why did he treat this Pharisee differently? What does this tell you about Nicodemus? What does it tell you about Jesus? What insight about mentoring can you learn from it?

3. Jesus laid out the gospel to Nicodemus and explained his desire to save people, not condemn them, but there is no explanation of the Pharisee's response. What do you think happened? Explain your answer.

_____

_____

_____

_____

_____

_____

_____

_____

_____

❸ Paul Mentors with Integrity

1 Thessalonians 2:1–20

[1] You know, brothers and sisters, that our visit to you was not without results. [2] We had previously suffered and been treated outrageously in Philippi, as you know, but with the help of our God we dared to tell you his gospel in the face of strong opposition. [3] For the appeal we make does not spring from error or impure motives, nor are we trying to trick you. [4] On the contrary, we speak as those approved by God to be entrusted with the gospel. We are not trying to please people but God, who tests our hearts. [5] You know we never used flattery, nor did we put on a mask to cover up greed—God is our witness. [6] We were not looking for praise from people, not from you or anyone else, even though as apostles of Christ we could have asserted our authority. [7] Instead, we were like young children among you.

Just as a nursing mother cares for her children, [8] so we cared for you. Because we loved you so much, we were delighted to share with you not only the gospel of God but our lives as well. [9] Surely you remember, brothers and sisters, our toil and hardship; we worked night and day in order not to be a burden to anyone while we preached the gospel of God to you. [10] You are witnesses, and so is God, of how holy, righteous and blameless we were among you who believed. [11] For you know that we dealt with each of you as a father deals with his own children, ¹² encouraging, comforting and urging you to live lives worthy of God, who calls you into his kingdom and glory.

¹³ And we also thank God continually because, when you received the word of God, which you heard from us, you accepted it not as a human word, but as it actually is, the word of God, which is indeed at work in you who believe. ¹⁴ For you, brothers and sisters, became imitators of God's churches in Judea, which are in Christ Jesus: You suffered from your own people the same things those churches suffered from the Jews ¹⁵ who killed the Lord Jesus and the prophets and also drove us out. They displease God and are hostile to everyone ¹⁶ in their effort to keep us from speaking to the Gentiles so that they may be saved. In this way they always heap up their sins to the limit. The wrath of God has come upon them at last.

¹⁷ But, brothers and sisters, when we were orphaned by being separated from you for a short time (in person, not in thought), out of our intense longing we made every effort to see you. ¹⁸ For we wanted to come to you— certainly I, Paul, did, again and again—but Satan blocked our way. ¹⁹ For what is our hope, our joy, or the crown in which we will glory in the presence of our Lord Jesus when he comes? Is it not you? ²⁰ Indeed, you are our glory and joy.

Study Questions

1. Paul says in this passage that he cared for the people in Thessalonica the way a nursing mother cares for her children. What do you think that means? How would you describe it?

_____

_____

_____

_____

_____

_____

_____

_____

2. Why do you think Paul and his companions worked hard not to be a burden to the people they were teaching? What lessons can you learn from this as a leader and mentor?

_____

_____

_____

_____

_____

_____

_____

3. What does Paul say about modeling in this passage? How is that important in mentoring? What does it do?

_____

_____

_____

_____

_____

_____

_____

_____

_____

4. What would you infer was Paul's reward for mentoring the Thessalonians? How does that knowledge affect you as a mentor and as someone to be mentored?

_____

_____

_____

_____

_____

_____

_____

_____

_____

LEADERSHIP INSIGHT AND REFLECTION

Based on your reading of the passages, how would you define the qualifications of a mentor? List them.

_____

_____

_____

_____

_____

_____

_____

_____

_____

What are the qualifications for someone who wants to be mentored?

_____

_____

_____

_____

_____

_____

_____

_____

What do you have to offer to people who might want to be mentored and developed by you? Who do you know who might be a candidate to be mentored? List their names.

_____

_____

_____

_____

_____

_____

_____

_____

In what areas do you most want to grow with the help of a mentor? Who do you know with the skills and experience who might be willing to mentor you?

_____

_____

_____

_____

_____

_____

_____

_____

_____

TAKING ACTION

Make two appointments—one with someone you'd like to ask to mentor you, and one with a candidate you'd like to mentor. When will you make the appointments?

Potential Mentor: _____

Potential Mentee: _____

Prepare for the meetings by writing any notes you'll need here.

Meeting 1

_____

_____

_____

_____

_____

Meeting 2

_____

_____

_____

_____

_____

GROUP DISCUSSION QUESTIONS

1. When Jesus said, "You Pharisees clean the outside of the cup and dish, but inside you are full of greed and wickedness," what do you think would have happened if they had admitted their wrongdoing, repented, and submitted to Jesus?

2. What would you identify as the single most important quality of a mentor?

3. What would you identify as the single most important quality of someone to be mentored?

4. What experience do you have in being mentored? What experience in mentoring others?

5. What did you find most rewarding about those experiences? What did you find most frustrating?

6. What dream do you have that you would be better positioned to accomplish if you were mentored? Who could help you with it? Are you willing to approach them and ask to be mentored?

7. Who could you help by being a mentor? How? Are you willing make that offer?

LESSON 18

DIVERSITY

Differences Can Be Made into a Strength

THE ISSUE DEFINED

The topic of diversity is not a simple one, and people have a wide variety of reactions to it. For some, it conjures images of demographic studies, awkward interactions, relational minefields, and diversity training sessions in the workplace. For others it represents good-old-boy networks, glass ceilings, and privilege. But good leaders see diversity as one of the best ways to build a world-class team. When properly led, motivated, and unleashed, a diverse group of professionals can gain an uncommon advantage over their competitors.

Differences really can make a difference on a team. But there is more to diversity than filling the team with unique individuals. In fact, diverse teams tend to heighten the leadership challenges. It's crucial for the leader to create an environment where differences are celebrated, and yet unity in the midst of those differences is encouraged.

Diverse teams bring together various personalities, skills, and experiences. Different personalities matter, because not everyone enjoys every type of task. Organizations need numbers people, sales people, idea people, and detail people. Different skills are equally important. Team members who have already been trained in human resources or project management are much better equipped to take on those roles. And variety in people's backgrounds and experiences enriches the entire team. When different perspectives are sought and shared, people on the team can find their common ground and learn to identify with each other. Empathy grows, and teamwork increases.

Wise leaders do more than gather a team that appears diverse on the surface. They continually get to know their people better, always uncovering the unique qualities that each one brings to the table. Effective leaders engage in conversations that draw out different perspectives, and they make it clear that they value independent thinking over flattery. They open up conversations, rather than shutting them down. And when leaders encourage and reward diversity, creativity, independent thinking, and open communication, they create a stimulating, challenging, and bold team. Everyone gets the most out of each other, and everyone wins.

CASE STUDIES

Read these case studies from the Bible and answer the study questions that follow.

❶ God Sets One Standard for Israelites and Foreigners

Numbers 15:1–2, 13–31

[1]The Lord said to Moses, [2] "Speak to the Israelites and say . . . [13] "'Everyone who is native-born must do these things in this way when they present a food offering as an aroma pleasing to the Lord. [14] For the generations to come, whenever a foreigner or anyone else living among you presents a food offering as an aroma pleasing to the Lord, they must do exactly as you do. [15] The community is to have the same rules for you and for the foreigner residing among you; this is a lasting ordinance for the generations to come. You and the foreigner shall be the same before the Lord: [16] The same laws and regulations will apply both to you and to the foreigner residing among you.'"

[17] The Lord said to Moses, [18] "Speak to the Israelites and say to them: 'When you enter the land to which I am taking you [19] and you eat the food of the land, present a portion as an offering to the Lord. [20] Present a loaf from the first of your ground meal and present it as an offering from the threshing floor. [21] Throughout the generations to come you are to give this offering to the Lord from the first of your ground meal.

22 "'Now if you as a community unintentionally fail to keep any of these commands the LORD gave Moses— 23 any of the LORD's commands to you through him, from the day the LORD gave them and continuing through the generations to come—24 and if this is done unintentionally without the community being aware of it, then the whole community is to offer a young bull for a burnt offering as an aroma pleasing to the LORD, along with its prescribed grain offering and drink offering, and a male goat for a sin offering. 25 The priest is to make atonement for the whole Israelite community, and they will be forgiven, for it was not intentional and they have presented to the LORD for their wrong a food offering and a sin offering. 26 The whole Israelite community and the foreigners residing among them will be forgiven, because all the people were involved in the unintentional wrong.

27 "'But if just one person sins unintentionally, that person must bring a year-old female goat for a sin offering. 28 The priest is to make atonement before the LORD for the one who erred by sinning unintentionally, and when atonement has been made, that person will be forgiven. 29 One and the same law applies to everyone who sins unintentionally, whether a native-born Israelite or a foreigner residing among you.

30 "'But anyone who sins defiantly, whether native-born or foreigner, blasphemes the LORD and must be cut off from the people of Israel. 31 Because they have despised the LORD's word and broken his commands, they must surely be cut off; their guilt remains on them.'"

Study Questions

1. As the descendants of Abraham, the Israelites are God's chosen people (Genesis 18:19), yet God includes foreigners in the instructions he gave to Moses for sacrifices. Why?

_____

_____

_____

_____

_____

_____

_____

2. What are the implications of the statement that the community of Israel-ites and the foreigners residing among them are to have the same rules, and that foreigners will be the same before the Lord as the Israelites? What does this tell you about God?

_____

_____

_____

_____

3. What are the implications of the statement, "This is a lasting ordinance for the generations to come" (verse 15)? How does this apply to believers today? How would you interpret the word *foreigner* in your current social and professional context?

_____

_____

_____

_____

❷ Unity Within Diversity

1 Corinthians 12:4–27

4 There are different kinds of gifts, but the same Spirit distributes them. 5 There are different kinds of service, but the same Lord. 6 There are different kinds of working, but in all of them and in everyone it is the same God at work.

7 Now to each one the manifestation of the Spirit is given for the common good. 8 To one there is given through the Spirit a message of wisdom, to another a message of knowledge by means of the same Spirit, 9 to another faith by the same Spirit, to another gifts of healing by that one Spirit, 10 to another miraculous powers, to another prophecy, to another distinguishing between spirits, to another speaking in different kinds of tongues, and to still another the interpretation of tongues. 11 All these are the work of one and the same Spirit, and he distributes them to each one, just as he determines.

¹² Just as a body, though one, has many parts, but all its many parts form one body, so it is with Christ. ¹³ For we were all baptized by one Spirit so as to form one body—whether Jews or Gentiles, slave or free—and we were all given the one Spirit to drink. ¹⁴ Even so the body is not made up of one part but of many.

¹⁵ Now if the foot should say, "Because I am not a hand, I do not belong to the body," it would not for that reason stop being part of the body. ¹⁶ And if the ear should say, "Because I am not an eye, I do not belong to the body," it would not for that reason stop being part of the body. ¹⁷ If the whole body were an eye, where would the sense of hearing be? If the whole body were an ear, where would the sense of smell be? ¹⁸ But in fact God has placed the parts in the body, every one of them, just as he wanted them to be. ¹⁹ If they were all one part, where would the body be? ²⁰ As it is, there are many parts, but one body.

²¹ The eye cannot say to the hand, "I don't need you!" And the head cannot say to the feet, "I don't need you!" ²² On the contrary, those parts of the body that seem to be weaker are indispensable, ²³ and the parts that we think are less honorable we treat with special honor. And the parts that are unpresentable are treated with special modesty, ²⁴ while our presentable parts need no special treatment. But God has put the body together, giving greater honor to the parts that lacked it, ²⁵ so that there should be no division in the body, but that its parts should have equal concern for each other. ²⁶ If one part suffers, every part suffers with it; if one part is honored, every part rejoices with it.

²⁷ Now you are the body of Christ, and each one of you is a part of it.

Study Questions

1. In this letter to the church at Corinth, Paul says that God gives "different kinds of gifts," "different kinds of service," and "different kinds of working" (which can be interpreted to mean *operations* or *results*) through the Holy Spirit. Why would God provide this diversity?

   _____

   _____

   _____

   _____

   _____

   _____

2. Why do you think Paul uses the human body as a metaphor for the diversity of skills and abilities among believers? What insights about teamwork and leadership can you gain from it?

_____

_____

_____

_____

_____

3. Paul deemphasizes the differences between Jews and Gentiles, slaves and free people, and says, "God has placed the parts in the body, every one of them, just as he wanted them to be" (verse 18). What kind of attitude should we have toward people who are different from us and play a different role?

_____

_____

_____

_____

_____

4. As you lead a team of people, what are the implications of Paul's statement, "If one part suffers, every part suffers with it" (verse 16)? How should this knowledge affect the way you lead?

_____

_____

_____

_____

❸ Paul Calls the Ephesians to a Higher Standard

Ephesians 4:1–16

1 As a prisoner for the Lord, then, I urge you to live a life worthy of the calling you have received. 2 Be completely humble and gentle; be patient, bearing with one another in love. 3 Make every effort to keep the unity of the Spirit through the bond of peace. *4 There is one body and one Spirit, just as you were called to one hope when you were called; *5 one Lord, one faith, one baptism; *6 one God and Father of all, who is over all and through all and in all.*

*7 But to each one of us grace has been given as Christ apportioned it. *8 This is why it says:*

> "When he ascended on high,
>   he took many captives
>   and gave gifts to his people."

*9 (What does "he ascended" mean except that he also descended to the lower, earthly regions? *10 He who descended is the very one who ascended higher than all the heavens, in order to fill the whole universe.) *11 So Christ himself gave the apostles, the prophets, the evangelists, the pastors and teachers, *12 to equip his people for works of service, so that the body of Christ may be built up *13 until we all reach unity in the faith and in the knowledge of the Son of God and become mature, attaining to the whole measure of the fullness of Christ.*

*14 Then we will no longer be infants, tossed back and forth by the waves, and blown here and there by every wind of teaching and by the cunning and craftiness of people in their deceitful scheming. *15 Instead, speaking the truth in love, we will grow to become in every respect the mature body of him who is the head, that is, Christ. *16 From him the whole body, joined and held together by every supporting ligament, grows and builds itself up in love, as each part does its work.*

Study Questions

1. What qualities does Paul cite in this letter to the Ephesians that should be used to help everyone maintain unity and work together?

   _____

   _____

   _____

   _____

   _____

2. What role does "speaking the truth in love" (verse 15) have in promoting diversity? What role does it have in maintaining unity?

_____

_____

_____

_____

_____

3. How is working together a sign of maturity, as described in the passage?

_____

_____

_____

_____

_____

LEADERSHIP INSIGHT AND REFLECTION

The passages in this lesson only scratched the surface in describing the many factors that make people different from one another. Review the passages and find as many of these factors as you can. List them here. Then add any other sources of diversity you can think of. Add them to the list.

_____

_____

_____

_____

_____

What are the challenges that come from these differences?

_____

_____

_____

_____

_____

What are the benefits of diversity? What is the role of leadership in working through the challenges and maximizing the benefits?

_____
_____
_____
_____
_____
_____

Taking Action

Where do you struggle when it comes to developing or maintaining unity while promoting diversity? Note which of them are internal and under your control.

_____
_____
_____
_____
_____
_____

What can you do to change and improve as a leader in this area? How would it benefit you and your team?

_____
_____
_____
_____
_____
_____

What will you commit to do? When will you do it?

_____
_____
_____
_____
_____

GROUP DISCUSSION QUESTIONS

1. When you read the passage from Numbers, which group do you naturally identify with: the Israelites or the foreigners? Why?

2. When you think of diversity, what immediately comes to mind? Being allowed into a group that wants to keep you out? Inviting in people from outside of your group? Adding people to your group or team with skills and experiences different from yours? Challenges and conflicts that inevitably arise from difference of opinion? A combination of these? Something different? Explain.

3. What stood out to you in the 1 Corinthians passage? What impact does it have on you? Were you surprised, convicted, instructed? Explain.

4. How can you translate the diversity and unity messages given for the body of Christ to a secular setting? What works well? What creates challenges?

5. What must leaders do to promote diversity? What must they do to promote unity?

6. Where have you fallen short when it comes to promoting diversity or unity?

7. What action do you believe God is asking you to take in your leadership so that you can grow in this area? When and how will you do it?

LESSON 19

CHANGE

You Must Lead Change to Improve Your Team

THE ISSUE DEFINED

Any person who has led change knows it's challenging. But I believe that people do not naturally resist change; they resist *being* changed. Recently I saw a two-frame cartoon in which the leader asks, "Who wants change?" and every hand is raised. But in the second frame, when he asks, "Who wants to change?" not one hand is raised. That pretty much characterizes human nature. We want the benefits of positive change without the pain of making any changes ourselves. Why is that?

People feel awkward and self-conscious doing something new. They are more comfortable with old problems than new solutions, because the new represents the unknown. Author and speaker Marilyn Ferguson put it this way: "It's not so much that we are afraid of change or so in love with the old ways, but it's that place in between that we fear. . . . It's like being between trapezes. It's Linus when his blanket is in the dryer. There's nothing to hold on to."

When people hear that change is coming, the first thing they do is ask, "How is this going to affect me?" Why? Because they are worried that they will have to give up something. Sometimes that question makes a lot of sense, such as when you're in danger of losing your job or your home. But most of the time, life is a series of trades anyway. Poet Ralph Waldo Emerson said, "For everything you gain, you lose something." So it's unrealistic to expect not to give up *anything*. However, many people are holding on so tightly to what they have that they are willing to forgo gaining anything—even progress. As leaders, we need to help people overcome this attitude.

People are afraid of being ridiculed, they personalize change, and they may feel alone in the process. Anyone who does something different always runs the risk of being mocked or ridiculed, and that can be a great deterrent to change. Most of the time when people experience change, particularly in businesses and organizations, they are not alone in the process, but they do often feel that way. And their emotions can overwhelm them. When anxiety rises, motivation falls. As leaders, we can become impatient and want them to get a grip and get over it. Instead, we need to show patience, acknowledge their humanness, and work with them. Not only will this help them process the change, but it will help us to influence them more quickly and move them forward.

Winston Churchill quipped, "To improve is to change, so to be perfect is to have changed often." Certainly we can't achieve perfection, but we can work to get as close as we can, and that means changing daily. As you work to keep the change message of progress alive with your people, talk about the change *clearly*, talk about the change *creatively*, and talk about the change *continually*.

In the end, your ability to create positive change will depend on whether the people you lead buy into you as a leader. You must use your credibility and influence to help others change when they *need to* so that they and the organization can best do what they *must do* to be successful.

CASE STUDIES

Read these case studies from the Bible and answer the study questions that follow.

❶ Naomi Encourages Ruth to Take a Huge Risk

Ruth 2:19–23

19 Her mother-in-law asked her, "Where did you glean today? Where did you work? Blessed be the man who took notice of you!"

Then Ruth told her mother-in-law about the one at whose place she had been working. "The name of the man I worked with today is Boaz," she said.

²⁰ "The LORD bless him!" Naomi said to her daughter-in-law. "He has not stopped showing his kindness to the living and the dead." She added, "That man is our close relative; he is one of our guardian-redeemers."

²¹ Then Ruth the Moabite said, "He even said to me, 'Stay with my workers until they finish harvesting all my grain.'"

²² Naomi said to Ruth her daughter-in-law, "It will be good for you, my daughter, to go with the women who work for him, because in someone else's field you might be harmed."

²³ So Ruth stayed close to the women of Boaz to glean until the barley and wheat harvests were finished. And she lived with her mother-in-law.

Ruth 3:1–18

¹ One day Ruth's mother-in-law Naomi said to her, "My daughter, I must find a home for you, where you will be well provided for. ² Now Boaz, with whose women you have worked, is a relative of ours. Tonight he will be winnowing barley on the threshing floor. ³ Wash, put on perfume, and get dressed in your best clothes. Then go down to the threshing floor, but don't let him know you are there until he has finished eating and drinking. ⁴ When he lies down, note the place where he is lying. Then go and uncover his feet and lie down. He will tell you what to do."

⁵ "I will do whatever you say," Ruth answered. ⁶ So she went down to the threshing floor and did everything her mother-in-law told her to do.

⁷ When Boaz had finished eating and drinking and was in good spirits, he went over to lie down at the far end of the grain pile. Ruth approached quietly, uncovered his feet and lay down. ⁸ In the middle of the night something startled the man; he turned—and there was a woman lying at his feet!

⁹ "Who are you?" he asked.

"I am your servant Ruth," she said. "Spread the corner of your garment over me, since you are a guardian-redeemer of our family."

¹⁰ "The LORD bless you, my daughter," he replied. "This kindness is greater than that which you showed earlier: You have not run after the younger men, whether rich or poor. ¹¹ And now, my daughter, don't be afraid. I will do for you all you ask. All the people of my town know that you are a woman of noble character.¹² Although it is true that I am a guardian-redeemer of our family, there is another who is more closely related than I. ¹³ Stay here for the night, and in the morning if he wants to do his duty as your guardian-redeemer, good; let him redeem you. But if he is not willing, as surely as the LORD lives I will do it. Lie here until morning."

¹⁴ So she lay at his feet until morning, but got up before anyone could be recognized; and he said, "No one must know that a woman came to the threshing floor."

¹⁵ He also said, "Bring me the shawl you are wearing and hold it out." When she did so, he poured into it six measures of barley and placed the bundle on her. Then he went back to town.

¹⁶ When Ruth came to her mother-in-law, Naomi asked, "How did it go, my daughter?"

Then she told her everything Boaz had done for her ¹⁷ and added, "He gave me these six measures of barley, saying, 'Don't go back to your mother-in-law empty-handed.'"

¹⁸ Then Naomi said, "Wait, my daughter, until you find out what happens. For the man will not rest until the matter is settled today."

Ruth 4:9–12

⁹ Then Boaz announced to the elders and all the people, "Today you are witnesses that I have bought from Naomi all the property of Elimelek, Kilion and Mahlon. ¹⁰ I have also acquired Ruth the Moabite, Mahlon's widow, as my wife, in order to maintain the name of the dead with his property, so that his name will not disappear from among his family or from his hometown. Today you are witnesses!"

¹¹ Then the elders and all the people at the gate said, "We are witnesses. May the Lord make the woman who is coming into your home like Rachel and Leah, who together built up the family of Israel. May you have standing in Ephrathah and be famous in Bethlehem. ¹² Through the offspring the Lord gives you by this young woman, may your family be like that of Perez, whom Tamar bore to Judah."

Study Questions

1. The widows had no one to support them, which was why Ruth was collecting food from the leftover grain after the harvest. Naomi recognized a need for change for them to survive. What does that say about Naomi's leadership?

_____

_____

_____

_____

_____

2. What opportunity did Naomi see for her daughter-in-law Ruth? What factors came into play in her ability to recognize it?

_____

_____

_____

_____

_____

3. How did Naomi prepare Ruth to seize the opportunity? What was the outcome?

_____

_____

_____

_____

_____

_____

2 Jesus Challenges People to Change

Matthew 5:17–48

17 "Do not think that I have come to abolish the Law or the Prophets; I have not come to abolish them but to fulfill them. 18 For truly I tell you, until heaven and earth disappear, not the smallest letter, not the least stroke of a pen, will by any means disappear from the Law until everything is accomplished. ¹⁹ Therefore anyone who sets aside one of the least of these commands and teaches others accordingly will be called least in the kingdom of heaven, but whoever practices and teaches these commands will be called great in the kingdom of heaven. ²⁰ For I tell you that unless your righteousness surpasses that of the Pharisees and the teachers of the law, you will certainly not enter the kingdom of heaven.

²¹ "You have heard that it was said to the people long ago, 'You shall not murder, and anyone who murders will be subject to judgment.' ²² But I tell you that anyone who is angry with a brother or sister will be subject to judgment. Again, anyone who says to a brother or sister, 'Raca,' is answerable to the court. And anyone who says, 'You fool!' will be in danger of the fire of hell.

²³ "Therefore, if you are offering your gift at the altar and there remember that your brother or sister has something against you, ²⁴ leave your gift there in front of the altar. First go and be reconciled to them; then come and offer your gift.

²⁵ "Settle matters quickly with your adversary who is taking you to court. Do it while you are still together on the way, or your adversary may hand you over to the judge, and the judge may hand you over to the officer, and you may be thrown into prison. ²⁶ Truly I tell you, you will not get out until you have paid the last penny.

²⁷ "You have heard that it was said, 'You shall not commit adultery.' ²⁸ But I tell you that anyone who looks at a woman lustfully has already committed adultery with her in his heart.²⁹ If your right eye causes you to stumble, gouge it out and throw it away. It is better for you to lose one part of your body than for your whole body to be thrown into hell. ³⁰ And if your right hand causes you to stumble, cut it off and throw it away. It is better for you to lose one part of your body than for your whole body to go into hell.

³¹ "It has been said, 'Anyone who divorces his wife must give her a certificate of divorce.' ³² But I tell you that anyone who divorces his wife, except for sexual immorality, makes her the victim of adultery, and anyone who marries a divorced woman commits adultery.

³³ "Again, you have heard that it was said to the people long ago, 'Do not break your oath, but fulfill to the Lord the vows you have made.' ³⁴ But I tell you, do not swear an oath at all: either by heaven, for it is God's throne; ³⁵ or by the earth, for it is his footstool; or by Jerusalem, for it is the city of the Great King. ³⁶ And do not swear by your head, for you cannot make even one hair white or black. ³⁷ All you need to say is simply 'Yes' or 'No'; anything beyond this comes from the evil one.

³⁸ "You have heard that it was said, 'Eye for eye, and tooth for tooth.' ³⁹ But I tell you, do not resist an evil person. If anyone slaps you on the right cheek, turn to them the other cheek also. ⁴⁰ And if anyone wants to sue you and take your shirt, hand over your coat as well. ⁴¹ If anyone forces you to go one mile, go with them two miles. ⁴² Give to the one who asks you, and do not turn away from the one who wants to borrow from you.

⁴³ "You have heard that it was said, 'Love your neighbor and hate your enemy.' ⁴⁴ But I tell you, love your enemies and pray for those who persecute you, ⁴⁵ that you may be children of your Father in heaven. He causes his sun to rise on the evil and the good, and sends rain on the righteous and the unrighteous. ⁴⁶ If you love those who love you, what reward will you get? Are not even the tax collectors doing that? ⁴⁷ And if you greet only your own people, what are you doing more than others? Do not even pagans do that? ⁴⁸ Be perfect, therefore, as your heavenly Father is perfect.

Study Questions

1. Why did Jesus first announce to everyone that he had come to fulfill the law and prophets, not abolish them? What was he doing by saying that?

_____

_____

_____

_____

_____

2. Examine Jesus's pattern of communication as he quoted the Old Testament and presented a change he wanted his followers to make. What can you learn from his communication?

_____

_____

_____

_____

_____

3. If you were asked to summarize the general principle of change that Jesus was communicating, how would you describe it? What are its implications to you as a follower of Christ?

_____

_____

_____

_____

_____

③ A Major Change for the Early Church

Acts 15:1–21

¹ Certain people came down from Judea to Antioch and were teaching the believers: "Unless you are circumcised, according to the custom taught by Moses, you cannot be saved." ² This brought Paul and Barnabas into sharp dispute and debate with them. So Paul and Barnabas were appointed, along with some other believers, to go up to Jerusalem to see the apostles and elders about this question. ³ The church sent them on their way, and as they traveled through Phoenicia and Samaria, they told how the Gentiles had been converted. This news made all the believers very glad. ⁴ When they came to Jerusalem, they were welcomed by the church and the apostles and elders, to whom they reported everything God had done through them.

⁵ Then some of the believers who belonged to the party of the Pharisees stood up and said, "The Gentiles must be circumcised and required to keep the law of Moses."

⁶ The apostles and elders met to consider this question. ⁷ After much discussion, Peter got up and addressed them: "Brothers, you know that some time ago God made a choice among you that the Gentiles might hear from my lips the message of the gospel and believe. ⁸ God, who knows the heart, showed that he accepted them by giving the Holy Spirit to them, just as he did to us. ⁹ He did not discriminate between us and them, for he purified their hearts by faith. ¹⁰ Now then, why do you try to test God by putting on the necks of Gentiles a yoke that neither we nor our ancestors have been able to bear? [11] *No! We believe it is through the grace of our Lord Jesus that we are saved, just as they are."*

[12] *The whole assembly became silent as they listened to Barnabas and Paul telling about the signs and wonders God had done among the Gentiles through them.* [13] *When they finished, James spoke up. "Brothers," he said, "listen to me.* [14] *Simon has described to us how God first intervened to choose a people for his name from the Gentiles.* [15] *The words of the prophets are in agreement with this, as it is written:*

> [16] *"'After this I will return*
> *and rebuild David's fallen tent.*
> *Its ruins I will rebuild,*
> *and I will restore it,*
> [17] *that the rest of mankind may seek the Lord,*
> *even all the Gentiles who bear my name,*
> *says the Lord, who does these things'—*
> [18] *things known from long ago.*

[19] *"It is my judgment, therefore, that we should not make it difficult for the Gentiles who are turning to God.* [20] *Instead we should write to them, telling them to abstain from food polluted by idols, from sexual immorality, from the meat of strangled animals and from blood.* [21] *For the law of Moses has been preached in every city from the earliest times and is read in the synagogues on every Sabbath."*

Study Questions

1. In what way were the believers who belonged to the party of the Pharisees resisting change? What do you think their motivation was? Explain.

_____

_____

_____

_____

_____

_____

2. How would you describe the communication that Peter used to counter the Pharisees' assertion? How would you characterize that of Barnabas and Paul? That of James? What can you learn from their approaches?

_____

_____

_____

_____

3. In the end, James made the decision on what would be done. What was his motivation for it?

_____

_____

_____

_____

Leadership Insight and Reflection

How did each of the leaders in these passages approach the process of creating change?

_____

_____

_____

_____

_____

_____

What challenges did each of them face? How did they overcome those challenges?

_____

_____

_____

_____

_____

_____

_____

_____

How do you handle change when others require it of you? Why do you react the way you do?

_____

_____

_____

_____

_____

As a leader, how do you handle change when guiding others through it? Are you strategic or impulsive? Are you persuasive or autocratic? Are you patient or impatient with people? Try to assess yourself honestly and impartially.

_____

_____

_____

_____

_____

TAKING ACTION

How do you need to change to become a better leader when it comes to leading change? Think through the process, and write your answer here.

_____

_____

_____

_____

_____

_____

_____

_____

_____

Look ahead. When is the next time you can put into practice the changes you will make?

_____

_____

GROUP DISCUSSION QUESTIONS

1. Naomi was a leader, yet she had no position, power, or status. How can leaders with those factors working against them facilitate change? What must they do that people with authority don't necessarily have to do?

2. Which of the six subjects Jesus spoke about in this passage struck you the most strongly: murder, adultery, divorce, oaths, retaliation, or loving enemies? Why?

3. How do you think the different groups who heard Jesus deliver this message responded? How do you think the Pharisees and teachers of the law responded? What about the crowds? What about Jesus's followers, including the disciples?

4. Are Jesus's words still a message of change? How are people responding today?

5. Why do you think Barnabas and Paul took the dispute about circumcision to Jerusalem for the apostles and elders? What implications for the church did the leaders' decision have?

6. Where do you most need to change when it comes to dealing with change?

7. What action do you believe God is asking you to take in your leadership growth as a result of this lesson? When and how will you do it?

LESSON 20

FAILURE

You Can Find a Lesson in Every Loss

THE ISSUE DEFINED

I believe the difference between average people and achieving people can be found in their perception of and response to failure. Why? Because there is no success without failure. Everyone fails, makes mistakes, and loses. These things are impossible to avoid or control. The only thing anyone can control is how they respond to failure. Leaders can achieve great things and profit from failure only when they both see it correctly and respond to it positively.

Perceiving failure as inevitable seems like it would create discouragement. But effective leaders also assume failure is temporary. They don't see a failure as an end, but rather a pause. Their perspective can be summed up in a quote that's often attributed to actress Gracie Allen: "Never place a period where God has placed a comma." After facing the reality of the mistake or failure, they choose to look beyond it to discover their next step. Wise leaders also choose not to see or define themselves by their failure. Their attitude is not, "This means I'm a failure." Instead, it's, "I did something that failed." The former belief feels permanent and inescapable. The latter embraces the lesson in the error, in order to avoid doing the same thing again. This makes failure useful.

Looking for the lesson in the loss is crucial. It's been said that experience is the best teacher. But in reality, we learn the most from *evaluated* experience.

Every failure has the potential to take us one step closer to success. Knowing what won't work is at least as important as knowing what will. Psychologist Joyce Brothers observed, "The person interested in success has to learn to view failure as a healthy, inevitable part of the process of getting to the top." Wisdom comes in learning to see failure as a milepost on the road of success.

This may sound ironic, but people who have experienced a lot of failure are actually in a better position to achieve success than people who haven't. When we fail, and fail, and fail again—and keep getting back up and learning—we build strength, tenacity, experience, and wisdom. And people who develop such qualities are capable of sustaining their success, unlike many for whom good things come early and easily. The key is to keep going and never give up. Most of the greatest wins in life came after a number of losses.

CASE STUDIES

Read these case studies from the Bible and answer the study questions that follow.

① God Meets Us at the Lowest Point

1 Kings 19:1–18

¹ Now Ahab told Jezebel everything Elijah had done and how he had killed all the prophets with the sword. ² So Jezebel sent a messenger to Elijah to say, "May the gods deal with me, be it ever so severely, if by this time tomorrow I do not make your life like that of one of them."

³ Elijah was afraid and ran for his life. When he came to Beersheba in Judah, he left his servant there, ⁴ while he himself went a day's journey into the wilderness. He came to a broom bush, sat down under it and prayed that he might die. "I have had enough, Lord," he said. "Take my life; I am no better than my ancestors." ⁵ Then he lay down under the bush and fell asleep.

All at once an angel touched him and said, "Get up and eat." ⁶ He looked around, and there by his head was some bread baked over hot coals, and a jar of water. He ate and drank and then lay down again.

⁷ The angel of the LORD came back a second time and touched him and said, "Get up and eat, for the journey is too much for you." ⁸ So he got up and ate and drank. Strengthened by that food, he traveled forty days and forty nights until he reached Horeb, the mountain of God. ⁹ There he went into a cave and spent the night.

And the word of the LORD came to him: "What are you doing here, Elijah?"

¹⁰ He replied, "I have been very zealous for the LORD God Almighty. The Israelites have rejected your covenant, torn down your altars, and put your prophets to death with the sword. I am the only one left, and now they are trying to kill me too."

¹¹ The LORD said, "Go out and stand on the mountain in the presence of the LORD, for the LORD is about to pass by."

Then a great and powerful wind tore the mountains apart and shattered the rocks before the LORD, but the LORD was not in the wind. After the wind there was an earthquake, but the LORD was not in the earthquake. ¹² After the earthquake came a fire, but the LORD was not in the fire. And after the fire came a gentle whisper. ¹³ When Elijah heard it, he pulled his cloak over his face and went out and stood at the mouth of the cave.

Then a voice said to him, "What are you doing here, Elijah?"

¹⁴ He replied, "I have been very zealous for the LORD God Almighty. The Israelites have rejected your covenant, torn down your altars, and put your prophets to death with the sword. I am the only one left, and now they are trying to kill me too."

¹⁵ The LORD said to him, "Go back the way you came, and go to the Desert of Damascus. When you get there, anoint Hazael king over Aram. ¹⁶ Also, anoint Jehu son of Nimshi king over Israel, and anoint Elisha son of Shaphat from Abel Meholah to succeed you as prophet. ¹⁷ Jehu will put to death any who escape the sword of Hazael, and Elisha will put to death any who escape the sword of Jehu.¹⁸ Yet I reserve seven thousand in Israel—all whose knees have not bowed down to Baal and whose mouths have not kissed him."

Study Questions

1. The chapter immediately before this passage describes a showdown between Elijah and the prophets of Baal, where God demonstrated his

supernatural power in response to Elijah's request, and then all Baal's prophets were executed. After such a great victory, why do you think Elijah ran away from Jezebel?

_____

_____

_____

_____

2. What did Elijah say that indicates he thought he had failed? What was his state of mind in response to it? Did he take it personally?

_____

_____

_____

_____

3. How did God respond to Elijah? Examining God's response, can you gain any insights about how to respond to feelings of failure?

_____

_____

_____

_____

4. Had Elijah really failed? What do you think? Explain.

_____

_____

_____

_____

❷ Failure Isn't Final

Lamentations 3:1–33

¹ I am the man who has seen affliction
by the rod of the LORD's wrath.

² *He has driven me away and made me walk*
    in darkness rather than light;
³ *indeed, he has turned his hand against me*
    again and again, all day long.

⁴ *He has made my skin and my flesh grow old*
    and has broken my bones.
⁵ *He has besieged me and surrounded me*
    with bitterness and hardship.
⁶ *He has made me dwell in darkness*
    like those long dead.

⁷ *He has walled me in so I cannot escape;*
    he has weighed me down with chains.
⁸ *Even when I call out or cry for help,*
    he shuts out my prayer.
⁹ *He has barred my way with blocks of stone;*
    he has made my paths crooked.

¹⁰ *Like a bear lying in wait,*
    like a lion in hiding,
¹¹ *he dragged me from the path and mangled me*
    and left me without help.
¹² *He drew his bow*
    and made me the target for his arrows.

¹³ *He pierced my heart*
    with arrows from his quiver.
¹⁴ *I became the laughingstock of all my people;*
    they mock me in song all day long.
¹⁵ *He has filled me with bitter herbs*
    and given me gall to drink.

¹⁶ *He has broken my teeth with gravel;*
    he has trampled me in the dust.
¹⁷ *I have been deprived of peace;*
    I have forgotten what prosperity is.

¹⁸ So I say, "My splendor is gone
and all that I had hoped from the Lord."

¹⁹ I remember my affliction and my wandering,
the bitterness and the gall.
²⁰ I well remember them,
and my soul is downcast within me.
²¹ Yet this I call to mind
and therefore I have hope:

²² Because of the Lord's great love we are not consumed,
for his compassions never fail.
²³ They are new every morning;
great is your faithfulness.
²⁴ I say to myself, "The Lord is my portion;
therefore I will wait for him."

²⁵ The Lord is good to those whose hope is in him,
to the one who seeks him;
²⁶ it is good to wait quietly
for the salvation of the Lord.
²⁷ It is good for a man to bear the yoke
while he is young.

²⁸ Let him sit alone in silence,
for the Lord has laid it on him.
²⁹ Let him bury his face in the dust—
there may yet be hope.
³⁰ Let him offer his cheek to one who would strike him,
and let him be filled with disgrace.

³¹ For no one is cast off
by the Lord forever.
³² Though he brings grief, he will show compassion,
so great is his unfailing love.
³³ For he does not willingly bring affliction
or grief to anyone.

Study Questions

1. In the beginning of this passage, the writer attributed his troubles to the Lord. What kinds of problems did he say he was experiencing? How did he say it made him feel?

_____

_____

_____

_____

_____

2. At the same time, the writer described many positive attributes belonging to the Lord. What are they? What do they say about God's character?

_____

_____

_____

_____

_____

3. How can someone be both positive and negative toward God at the same time? Have you ever felt that way? Why would the writer choose to wait on God despite how he felt?

_____

_____

_____

_____

_____

❸ Two Failures, Two Different Reactions

Matthew 26:14–16, 31–35

¹⁴ Then one of the Twelve—the one called Judas Iscariot—went to the chief priests ¹⁵ and asked, "What are you willing to give me if I deliver him over to you?" So they counted out for him thirty pieces of silver. 16 From then on Judas watched for an opportunity to hand him over. . . .

31 Then Jesus told them, "This very night you will all fall away on account of me, for it is written:

"'I will strike the shepherd,
and the sheep of the flock will be scattered.'

32 But after I have risen, I will go ahead of you into Galilee."

33 Peter replied, "Even if all fall away on account of you, I never will."

34 "Truly I tell you," Jesus answered, "this very night, before the rooster crows, you will disown me three times."

35 But Peter declared, "Even if I have to die with you, I will never disown you." And all the other disciples said the same.

Matthew 26:69–75

69 Now Peter was sitting out in the courtyard, and a servant girl came to him. "You also were with Jesus of Galilee," she said.

70 But he denied it before them all. "I don't know what you're talking about," he said.

71 Then he went out to the gateway, where another servant girl saw him and said to the people there, "This fellow was with Jesus of Nazareth."

72 He denied it again, with an oath: "I don't know the man!"

73 After a little while, those standing there went up to Peter and said, "Surely you are one of them; your accent gives you away."

74 Then he began to call down curses, and he swore to them, "I don't know the man!"

Immediately a rooster crowed. 75 Then Peter remembered the word Jesus had spoken: "Before the rooster crows, you will disown me three times." And he went outside and wept bitterly.

Matthew 27:1–5

1 Early in the morning, all the chief priests and the elders of the people made their plans how to have Jesus executed. 2 So they bound him, led him away and handed him over to Pilate the governor.

³ When Judas, who had betrayed him, saw that Jesus was condemned, he was seized with remorse and returned the thirty pieces of silver to the chief priests and the elders. ⁴ "I have sinned," he said, "for I have betrayed innocent blood."

"What is that to us?" they replied. "That's your responsibility."

⁵ So Judas threw the money into the temple and left. Then he went away and hanged himself.

Study Questions

1. Judas and Peter both failed Jesus, Judas by delivering Jesus to the chief priests to be arrested and Peter by disowning Jesus after he was arrested. How did each of them react to their failure? What does it say about them?

_____

_____

_____

_____

_____

2. Which of the men do you think fell further: the one who boasted he would be faithful but wasn't, or the one who said nothing but did wrong? Explain.

_____

_____

_____

_____

3. John 21 contains Jesus's interaction with Peter where Peter said he loved Jesus and was restored. Judas repented to the priests, but they showed him no mercy. What do you think would have happened to Judas if he had lived, repented to Jesus, and asked for forgiveness?

_____

_____

_____

_____

_____

LEADERSHIP INSIGHT AND REFLECTION

In your opinion, how much of what Elijah considered a failure was due to his perception of his situation and how much was based on facts? What does this tell you about failure, how people interpret it, and what they do in response?

_____
_____
_____
_____
_____
_____
_____

Based on your reading of the three passages, who ultimately determines whether or not someone has actually failed? How does that impact your perception and treatment of failure?

_____
_____
_____
_____
_____
_____
_____
_____

As a leader, how should you handle your own failures? How should you handle the failure of others on your team? What should you be attempting to accomplish in both cases?

_____
_____
_____
_____
_____
_____
_____

TAKING ACTION

How well have you handled failures by yourself and others? How would you rate yourself on a scale of 1 (low) to 10 (high) in each area? What do you do well? What do you do poorly?

_____

_____

_____

_____

_____

_____

_____

_____

_____

_____

_____

_____

What specific action can you take to improve? When will you do it?

_____

_____

_____

_____

_____

_____

_____

_____

_____

_____

_____

_____

GROUP DISCUSSION QUESTIONS

1. Elijah is considered to be one of the greatest prophets of the Old Testament. What does his behavior teach you about failure and discouragement?

2. In the passage from Lamentations, the writer at first blames God for his problems. When things go wrong for you, where are you most likely to place the blame? Why?

3. You read the Lamentations writer's opinion of God. What characteristics do you attribute to him? How does your description compare to the writer of Lamentations?

4. What do you think Peter learned from his denial of Jesus? How do you think it impacted the way he later lived and led others?

5. Are you more likely to attempt boldly and fail or be more conservative and succeed? Why do you think you are the way you are?

6. How has that inclination affected your success and your leadership?

7. How do you think God would want you to change in this area? What are you willing to do? When and how will you do it?

POWER

The Best Use of Leadership Is Serving Others

THE ISSUE DEFINED

You've probably heard the saying, "Power corrupts. And absolute power corrupts absolutely." That can be true. But I believe the abuse of power happens on a continuum. The temptation toward corruption or abuse grows as power increases. Very few leaders leap from zero power to absolute power—and the absolute corruption it can bring. The reality is that power (in other words, influence) does not automatically result in pitfalls like corruption. But as leaders increase in influence, the temptations that come with power do increase at the same rate. And they must be actively combatted.

The first pitfall of increasing power is selfishness, so good leaders must fight to focus on the higher calling of serving others. Many leaders begin their pursuit of power out of selfish motives, and they use it selfishly as well. But even the most well-meaning servant leaders can be seduced by power—gradually, as they enjoy the perks, they fall into focusing on their own desires first. Wise leaders fight this temptation by habitually taking a genuine interest in the people they lead. When you build relationships with followers, learn about their hopes and dreams, and focus on helping them to reach their potential, you are more likely to seek their benefit first.

Arrogance is another temptation of power. Leaders can start to think that everything is all about them, and that they deserve what they get—especially when the team or organization is winning. The way to fight this is to continually check their ego.

Wise leaders cultivate humility and gratitude daily, by giving credit to God for their blessings and to other people for their successes. When leaders remain humble, they are less likely to act entitled or demanding. They hold loosely to their power.

Another thing that leaders must hold loosely is comfort. One of the greatest temptations of power is to chase comfort and wealth. Greater success creates greater income, which can provide increased comfort (with a bigger house, a nicer car, more creature comforts). And the more comfortable humans are, the more comfort they want to have. At that point, many leaders start chasing comfort, and the money needed to obtain it. And while money itself is not evil, its pursuit is.

The antidote to this pursuit is contentment. And it must be chased with the same enthusiasm. Wise leaders strive to increase their contentment in all circumstances (Philippians 4:11). Leaders who are content have more peace and practice more generosity. As they gain more, they give more.

Wise leaders know that power is tremendously seductive, and as it increases, so does their risk of giving in to its temptations. They are well aware that they can't trust themselves. So they do more than fight the perils of power on their own; they make themselves transparent and accountable to others. Only with those safeguards and constant vigilance can leaders hope to avoid the corruption of power.

CASE STUDIES

Read these case studies from the Bible and answer the study questions that follow.

❶ Rehoboam Chooses Power Over Wisdom

2 Chronicles 10:1–19

¹ Rehoboam went to Shechem, for all Israel had gone there to make him king. ² When Jeroboam son of Nebat heard this (he was in Egypt, where he had fled from King Solomon), he returned from Egypt. ³ So they sent for Jeroboam, and he and all Israel went to Rehoboam and said to him: ⁴ "Your father put a heavy yoke on us, but now lighten the harsh labor and the heavy yoke he put on us, and we will serve you."

⁵ Rehoboam answered, "Come back to me in three days." So the people went away.

⁶ Then King Rehoboam consulted the elders who had served his father Solomon during his lifetime. "How would you advise me to answer these people?" he asked.

⁷ They replied, "If you will be kind to these people and please them and give them a favorable answer, they will always be your servants."

⁸ But Rehoboam rejected the advice the elders gave him and consulted the young men who had grown up with him and were serving him. ⁹ He asked them, "What is your advice? How should we answer these people who say to me, 'Lighten the yoke your father put on us'?"

¹⁰ The young men who had grown up with him replied, "The people have said to you, 'Your father put a heavy yoke on us, but make our yoke lighter.' Now tell them, 'My little finger is thicker than my father's waist. ¹¹ My father laid on you a heavy yoke; I will make it even heavier. My father scourged you with whips; I will scourge you with scorpions.'"

¹² Three days later Jeroboam and all the people returned to Rehoboam, as the king had said, "Come back to me in three days." ¹³ The king answered them harshly. Rejecting the advice of the elders, ¹⁴ he followed the advice of the young men and said, "My father made your yoke heavy; I will make it even heavier. My father scourged you with whips; I will scourge you with scorpions." ¹⁵ So the king did not listen to the people, for this turn of events was from God, to fulfill the word the Lord had spoken to Jeroboam son of Nebat through Ahijah the Shilonite.

¹⁶ When all Israel saw that the king refused to listen to them, they answered the king:

> *"What share do we have in David,*
>   *what part in Jesse's son?*
> *To your tents, Israel!*
>   *Look after your own house, David!"*

So all the Israelites went home. ¹⁷ But as for the Israelites who were living in the towns of Judah, Rehoboam still ruled over them.

¹⁸ King Rehoboam sent out Adoniram, who was in charge of forced labor, but the Israelites stoned him to death. King Rehoboam, however, managed to get into his chariot and escape to Jerusalem. ¹⁹ *So Israel has been in rebellion against the house of David to this day.*

Study Questions

1. Rehoboam was made king after his father Solomon died. What was his mindset as he received the power of the throne for the first time?

_____

_____

_____

_____

_____

_____

_____

2. How did the elders advise him when the people asked for him to treat them less harshly? How did they tell him to treat the people of Israel? What did they say would be the result of the treatment they advised?

_____

_____

_____

_____

_____

_____

3. Why do you think Rehoboam rejected that advice and sought the advice of others? Why didn't the elders' advice appeal to him? What did Rehoboam want? What does his remark about his finger being thicker than his father's waist tell you about him?

_____

_____

_____

_____

_____

_____

4. Why had the people of Israel tolerated Solomon's heavy yoke? Why didn't they submit to Rehoboam? What leadership lesson can you learn from this?

_____

_____

_____

_____

② The Power of Riches Never Satisfies

Ecclesiastes 5:8–20

8 If you see the poor oppressed in a district, and justice and rights denied, do not be surprised at such things; for one official is eyed by a higher one, and over them both are others higher still. 9 The increase from the land is taken by all; the king himself profits from the fields.

10 Whoever loves money never has enough;
_   whoever loves wealth is never satisfied with their income._
_   This too is meaningless._
11 As goods increase,
_   so do those who consume them._
_   And what benefit are they to the owners_
_   except to feast their eyes on them?_
12 The sleep of a laborer is sweet,
_   whether they eat little or much,_
_   but as for the rich, their abundance_
_   permits them no sleep._

13 I have seen a grievous evil under the sun:

_   wealth hoarded to the harm of its owners,_
_   14 or wealth lost through some misfortune,_
_   so that when they have children_
_   there is nothing left for them to inherit._

¹⁵ Everyone comes naked from their mother's womb,
  and as everyone comes, so they depart.
They take nothing from their toil
  that they can carry in their hands.

¹⁶ This too is a grievous evil:

  As everyone comes, so they depart,
    and what do they gain,
      since they toil for the wind?
¹⁷ All their days they eat in darkness,
    with great frustration, affliction and anger.

¹⁸ This is what I have observed to be good: that it is appropriate for a person to eat, to drink and to find satisfaction in their toilsome labor under the sun during the few days of life God has given them—for this is their lot. ¹⁹ Moreover, when God gives someone wealth and possessions, and the ability to enjoy them, to accept their lot and be happy in their toil—this is a gift of God. ²⁰ They seldom reflect on the days of their life, because God keeps them occupied with gladness of heart.

Study Questions

1. Why does the writer of Ecclesiastes say that we should not be surprised when we see the poor oppressed and justice denied to people? What does this say about human nature and what often happens when people receive position and power?

   _____

   _____

   _____

   _____

   _____

   _____

   _____

   _____

2. According to the writer of this passage, what do wealth and possessions do for us? What can we take with us when we depart from this life? What should we learn from this knowledge?

_____

_____

_____

_____

_____

_____

_____

_____

3. The passage suggests that God alone has the power to give wealth, possessions, and worthy work. What should our attitude toward him be?

_____

_____

_____

_____

_____

_____

_____

4. Given the insight that those who pursue wealth and possessions are never satisfied with what they gain, why do people still dedicate themselves to them? How can we guard against doing this ourselves?

_____

_____

_____

_____

_____

_____

_____

③ The Nature of Real Power

Matthew 20:20–28

²⁰ Then the mother of Zebedee's sons came to Jesus with her sons and, kneeling down, asked a favor of him.

²¹ "What is it you want?" he asked.

She said, "Grant that one of these two sons of mine may sit at your right and the other at your left in your kingdom."

²² "You don't know what you are asking," Jesus said to them. "Can you drink the cup I am going to drink?"

"We can," they answered.

²³ Jesus said to them, "You will indeed drink from my cup, but to sit at my right or left is not for me to grant. These places belong to those for whom they have been prepared by my Father."

²⁴ When the ten heard about this, they were indignant with the two brothers. ²⁵ Jesus called them together and said, "You know that the rulers of the Gentiles lord it over them, and their high officials exercise authority over them. ²⁶ Not so with you. Instead, whoever wants to become great among you must be your servant, ²⁷ and whoever wants to be first must be your slave— ²⁸ just as the Son of Man did not come to be served, but to serve, and to give his life as a ransom for many."

Study Questions

1. What was the mother of James and John really asking for in this passage? Why do you think she made her request?

_____

_____

_____

_____

_____

_____

_____

_____

2. When Jesus asked, "Can you drink the cup I am going to drink?" what was he saying about responsibility and how it relates to power?

_____

_____

_____

_____

_____

_____

_____

3. According to Jesus, what is an improper use of power? What is a proper use?

_____

_____

_____

_____

_____

_____

LEADERSHIP INSIGHT AND REFLECTION

Many people believe Ecclesiastes was written by King Solomon. Compare that writing's perspective on power with what you read about Rehoboam, Solomon's son. How do their attitudes differ? What didn't Rehoboam learn from his father?

_____

_____

_____

_____

_____

_____

_____

_____

_____

_____

Compare what Jesus said about power in the Mark passage with what's written in the Ecclesiastes passage. How do they differ? How much of the contrast between them could be attributed to the difference between human and divine perspectives?

_____

_____

_____

_____

_____

_____

_____

In what areas of your life do you have power? How do you use it? Based on what you've read in this lesson, how do you think God would desire for you to use it?

_____

_____

_____

_____

_____

_____

_____

Taking Action

What do you believe God wants you to accomplish with the power you have? Do you need more power or influence to accomplish it? Based on your past track record, can you be trusted with more power or influence? Have you been faithful and trustworthy with the power you've already received? Explain.

_____

_____

_____

_____

_____

_____

_____

Where do you need to grow in your use of power and influence so that you are more consistent with God's teaching?

_____
_____
_____
_____
_____
_____
_____
_____
_____
_____
_____

What will you do? When will you do it? Who will you invite to hold you accountable?

_____
_____
_____
_____
_____
_____
_____
_____
_____
_____
_____

Group Discussion Questions

1. What were the motivations of the two groups who advised Rehoboam: (1) the elders, and (2) the young men who grew up with Rehoboam and served him?

2. What filters have you put into place for judging the advice you receive from others? Do you need to give more consideration to others' desire for power?

3. How is the acquisition and use of power impacted by a leader's motives?

4. How are power and money related? Are either inherently bad? How does love for them come into play?

5. The passage from Matthew says, "When the ten heard about this, they were indignant with the two brothers" (verse 24). Why were they upset?

6. Why is it so difficult for human beings to use power for unselfish service?

7. How do you need to change the way you use the power you have to become more like Christ? What will you do to improve? When and how will you do it?

FINAL GROUP DISCUSSION QUESTIONS

I recommend that you meet together with your group one additional time after you finish the lesson on power. Before the meeting, ask everyone to take some time to reflect on the entire leadership development process they've gone through. Then when you meet, answer the following questions.

1. How would you describe your leadership journey since you started this process?

2. Have you taken on a greater leadership role or been more proactive as a leader since studying the 21 leadership issues in the Bible? If so, how? If not, why not?

3. What issue or problem were you able to solve as a result of the work you did in this study guide? How did what you learned from the Bible help you?

4. Which of the issues do you find the most challenging to you personally as a leader? Why do you struggle in this area?

5. Have you made any big-picture changes in your leadership philosophy or your approach to leading others as a result of what you've learned? Explain.

6. Are others responding to you differently as a leader than in the past? If so, how?

7. What is your single greatest takeaway from this study?

8. What did you learn from others in the group?

9. Where do you most want to grow next in your leadership?

ABOUT THE AUTHOR

John C. Maxwell is a #1 *New York Times* bestselling author, coach, and speaker who has sold more than thirty million books in fifty languages. He has been identified as the #1 leader in business by the American Management Association and the most influential leadership expert in the world by *Business Insider* and *Inc.* magazines. He is the founder of the John Maxwell Company, the John Maxwell Team, EQUIP, and the John Maxwell Leadership Foundation, organizations that have trained millions of leaders from every country of the world. The recipient of the Mother Teresa Prize for Global Peace and Leadership from the Luminary Leadership Network, Dr. Maxwell speaks each year to Fortune 500 companies, presidents of nations, and many of the world's top business leaders. He can be followed at Twitter.com/JohnCMaxwell. For more information about him, visit JohnMaxwell.com.

LEADERSHIP
FOUNDATION

transforming
LEADERS
transforming
COUNTRIES

Together,
WE CAN CHANGE THE WORLD.
jmlf.org

THE JOHN MAXWELL
L E A D E R S H I P
P O D C A S T

MAXIMIZE YOUR GROWTH EVERY WEEK WITH JOHN AND HIS INNER CIRCLE.

SUBSCRIBE NOW to hear from John and CEO of The John Maxwell Enterprise, Mark Cole, as they unpack the practical applications of John's timeless teachings and give you actionable ways to apply them to your life and work.

SUBSCRIBE NOW AT **MAXWELLPODCAST.COM**

ALSO AVAILABLE ON

GREATER INFLUENCE, IMPACT AND INCOME.

The JOHN MAXWELL **Team**

Visit
JMTinfo.com
today!

It's time to make the
SHIFT!

If you've ever dreamed of building your career
as a coach, consultant, speaker or trainer, it's time to shift
between where you are and where you want to be.

Maybe you're thinking of a career pivot, or perhaps you coach, consult, or speak regularly and want to level up your business with better clients, bigger opportunities, and more impact.

The John Maxwell Team will give you:

» Clarity you need to step into your best season of life.
» Key insights you need to break through barriers to growth and unlock your potential.
» Instant authority that positions you for better work and bigger opportunities.
» A rich, thriving community that challenges, inspires, and encourages you.
» Exclusive rights to John Maxwell content for your organization or career development.

Go to <u>JMTinfo.com</u> to speak to one of my Program Coordinators today.

To your success,
John

THE JOHN MAXWELL LEADERSHIP BLOG

Every week John Maxwell
and CEO of The John Maxwell Enterprise, Mark Cole,
share their in-the-moment thoughts on leadership
and how to navigate your personal growth journey
week by week.

CHECK IT OUT AT **JOHNMAXWELL.COM/BLOG**

**THINKING
LIKE A LEADER**

The Top 10 Truths Everyone Must Know
about The 5 Levels of Leadership

Co.

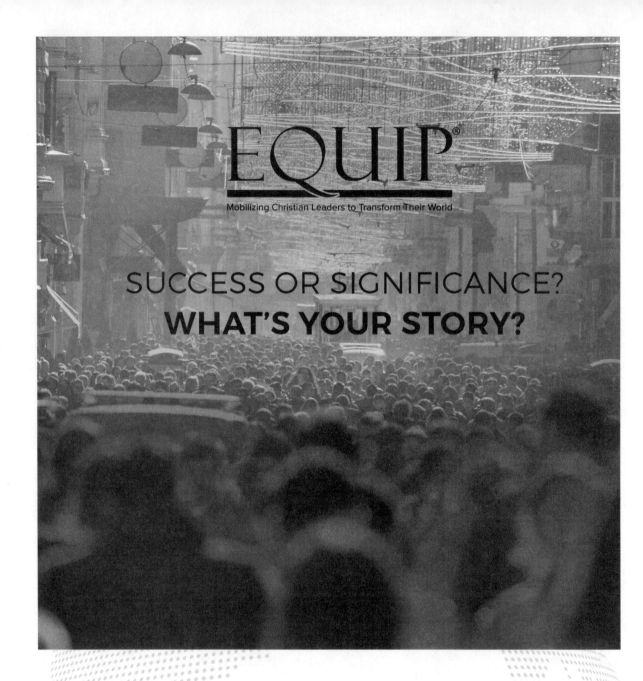

SUCCESS OR SIGNIFICANCE?
WHAT'S YOUR STORY?

MOBILIZING LEADERS FOR
TRANSFORMATION

iequip.church | 678.225.3300